CONVERGING PATHS TO RESTRICTION:
FRENCH, ITALIAN, AND BRITISH RESPONSES TO IMMIGRATION

DEMETRIOS G. PAPADEMETRIOU
AND KIMBERLY A. HAMILTON

INTERNATIONAL MIGRATION POLICY PROGRAM
CARNEGIE ENDOWMENT FOR INTERNATIONAL PEACE

© 1996 by the
Carnegie Endowment for International Peace
2400 N Street, N.W.
Washington, D.C. 20037
Tel. (202) 862-7900
Fax (202) 862-2610

All rights reserved. No part of this publication may be reproduced or transmitted in any form or by any means without permission in writing from the Carnegie Endowment.

Converging Paths to Restriction: French, Italian, and British Responses to Immigration
(ISBN 0-87003-073-6/$6.95)
may be ordered from:
The Brookings Institution
Department 029
Washington, D.C. 20041-0029, USA
Tel. 1-800-275-1447 or 202-797-6258.
Fax 202-797-6004.

Cover and series design: Paddy McLaughlin Concepts & Design.
Printed by Automated Graphic Systems.

The Carnegie Endowment for International Peace normally does not take institutional positions on public policy issues; the views and recommendations presented in this publication do not necessarily represent the views of the Carnegie Endowment, its officers, staff, or trustees.

CONTENTS

Preface ... 1

1. INTRODUCTION ... 3

2. FRANCE: IMMIGRATION RECONSIDERED ... 5
The Historical Backdrop ... 6
The Post-1974 Period: The Fictitious Halt ... 7
The Dilemmas of Labor Immigration ... 11
The Challenge of Unauthorized Employment ... 14
New Directions in Asylum ... 15
Citizenship and Ethnicity: *Nos Ancêtres les Gaulois?* ... 19
Immigration, Cultural Distance, and Islam ... 24
Education and Immigration ... 26
The State Responds: Ambivalence and Misunderstanding ... 28
Internal and External Dimensions ... 29
Understanding the Debate ... 32

3. ITALY: COMING TO TERMS WITH "RECEIVING" COUNTRY STATUS ... 39
The Tumultuous Context ... 46
Institutional Responses and Changing Flows ... 48
Toward Increasing Sophistication in Policy and Management ... 53

4. THE UNITED KINGDOM: THE RELENTLESS SEARCH FOR MINIMIZING IMMIGRATION ... 55
Safeguarding Sovereign Prerogatives vis-à-vis Brussels ... 59
Settlement Issues, Labor Migration, and Asylum ... 60
British Immigration Policies ... 62
Deterring Asylum Claims ... 64
Tightening Naturalization and Citizenship Requirements ... 68
Britain's Troubled Race and Ethnic Relations ... 69
Persistent Patterns and Policies ... 72

5. CONCLUSION: TRENDS AND LESSONS ... 75

REFERENCES ... 79

About the Authors ... 87

About the Carnegie Endowment for International Peace and the International Migration Policy Program ... 88

Other Studies in this Series ... 91

PREFACE

This paper is the third in the series on international migration and refugee policy issues published by the International Migration Policy Program of the Carnegie Endowment for International Peace. Together with two forthcoming studies examining the European Union's search for a *European* policy response to migration and Germany's extraordinary effort to manage the competing demands and tensions that arise from migration, *Converging Paths to Restriction* forms part of a trilogy that critiques Western Europe's responses to migration on the eve of the 21st Century.

The migration issue has become too complex to address effectively without relying extensively on the written and unwritten perspectives and ideas of others—more so than even the most complete referencing can hope to document. Demetrios Papademetriou would therefore like to acknowledge his intellectual debt to his colleagues in the many meetings held under the auspices of the Organisation for Economic Co-operation and Development (OECD): the OECD's Migration Working Party, on which he has served since 1988 and which he has had the privilege of chairing since 1992; the technical experts' discussions associated with the Continuous Reporting System on Migration (better known by its French acronym, SOPEMI), on which he served from 1988 to 1992 and which he continues to attend whenever an opportunity to do so arises; and the three hugely successful conferences on these issues (in Rome in 1991, Madrid in 1994, and Tokyo in 1995). All have proven to be extraordinary educational opportunities. Formal and less formal conversations with public officials and analysts on these same issues over the years have served a similar role.

Kimberly Hamilton would like to thank the French National Institute of Demographic Studies (INED) and Professor Jean-Claude Chesnais for a three-month residency in 1994 that allowed her to study French immigration intensively.

Both authors would also like to thank Gerard Moreau, John Salt, and Patrick Weil, as well as our Carnegie colleagues Morton Abramowitz, Lynne Davidson, and Valeriana Kallab for taking the time to read and critique various versions of the manuscript. Credit and thanks for most of the editing go to Patricia W. Blair.

We owe a heartfelt debt to our senior partner in the International Migration Policy Program, Kathleen Newland, who patiently took time from her own busy schedule to provide a key critical eye and thoughtful suggestions, which have improved the manuscript.

We acknowledge gratefully the invaluable research assistance of Yasmin Santiago (who also guided and managed the manuscript from its inception to its publication), Carolina Bahr, Maryam Kamali Miyamoto, and Nikhilesh Korgaonkar. Violet Lee patiently typed several versions of the manuscript.

Finally, as it is both proper and customary to acknowledge, any errors of commission or omission rest squarely with the authors.

1. INTRODUCTION

ost of the governments of Europe are moving swiftly to tighten their immigration and asylum policies. In this struggle to respond to the pressures of international migration, two processes have commanded the lion's share of attention: Germany's determined efforts to reduce immigration from and through Eastern Europe, and the efforts of the European Union (EU) to forge a continent-wide policy framework to suit the restrictionist mood of the member states.[1] These highly visible processes have tended to obscure the fact that other European countries are also pressing forward with their own independent efforts to achieve sharply reduced entries. These differ greatly from one country to another in character and in impact, but are consistent with the ideas and policies pursued by Germany and the EU. Collectively, they may be even more important.

This essay focuses on how France, Italy, and the United Kingdom have been responding to the difficult social, cultural, political, and economic policy issues raised by immigration, refugee, and asylum matters. The paths they have chosen reflect different historical patterns of labor recruitment, foreign policy priorities, and attitudes toward immigration and citizenship. In the case of Italy, a crippled political system's halting attempts to deal with a relatively new challenge are also a factor. Nonetheless, the three countries' paths are unmistakably converging toward increasing restriction and intolerance.

---

[1] These two processes are examined in depth in two forthcoming Carnegie Endowment publications. See Papademetriou 1996 and Papademetriou with Kamali Miyamoto 1996.

In France, historical links with the countries of the Maghreb color a contentious debate over the interrelationships among immigration, Islam, and domestic political stability—in a period when successive French governments have tried to respond to the political and social consequences of economic restructuring and persistent high unemployment. Italy, in a period of political upheaval, faces new immigration challenges as a result of its swift and dramatic transformation from one of Europe's major "sending" countries to a significant "receiving" one. Recent governments of the United Kingdom (U.K.)—fully convinced of immigration's socially destabilizing effects—maintain strict limits on immigration and refuse to cede policy responsibility for border controls to the European Union.

Controlling unauthorized immigration and further restricting the admission of immigrants, refugees, and asylum seekers are not the only objectives of the governments of the three countries examined. France, the U.K., and (to a lesser degree) Italy are also engaged in divisive internal debates over how to integrate their immigrant communities. Longstanding policies have come under increasing scrutiny. Immigration and refugee issues now intrude regularly into electoral politics, despite efforts by mainstream political parties to prevent this. A rocky path lies ahead as Europe's governments and supranational institutions ponder a range of policy options to deal with newcomers.

It is important to note that these three countries' perceptions of the migration challenge and the tenor of their responses to it are in many ways representative of other Western and Northern European countries. France's attempts to address the social and cultural challenges associated with immigration, its increasing preoccupation with South-to-North migration, and its continuing commitment to (if decreasing enthusiasm for) the European Union parallel the concerns of several other EU member states. Italy's struggle to come to terms with its new status as a major transit and receiving country for immigrants has much in common with the dilemmas faced by Spain, Greece, and Austria. Finally, the U.K.'s views about immigration and asylum and its resolute opposition to transferring authority over these issues to EU institutions in Brussels represent positions quietly shared by other members, including Denmark and Greece. Thus the countries examined in this essay, along with Germany, to a large extent represent advanced industrial Europe's fears and hopes about migration issues.

2. FRANCE: IMMIGRATION RECONSIDERED

New directions in France's immigration and asylum policy became apparent shortly after Edouard Balladur became Prime Minister in March 1993. In May 1993, Charles Pasqua, the new Interior Minister, introduced a bill on the control of immigration and the conditions for foreigners' entry into and residence in France (the Pasqua Law).[2] The proposal—which initially set a goal of "zero immigration" (Weil 1994), but was quickly "clarified" to mean zero *illegal* immigration following protests from, among others, Simone Veil, the French Minister for Social, Health, and Urban Affairs—represented a fundamental retreat in French official views toward immigration.[3] A bill on "the control of immigration" was first approved in August 1993. Following the rejection of some of that bill's provisions by France's *Conseil d' État*, a second bill was approved in December 1993—after a lengthy battle that also reflected the EU's supranational pull on France by incorporating the constitutional changes necessary for French participation in two EU immigration control arrangements, the Schengen Agreement and the Dublin Convention.[4]

---

[2]This was the second time that Pasqua entered the immigration fray in a significant way. He had pursued a similar agenda in the late 1980s, when the Center-Right briefly held power. His policies were repudiated in 1989, following François Mitterrand's re-election and the Socialists' return to power.

[3]The replacement of the Balladur government by a government headed by Alain Juppé (following Jacques Chirac's election to the French Presidency in May 1995) does not seem to have led to any change in direction on immigration. The new Interior Minister, Jean Louis Debré, has further increased employer costs of hiring illegal workers (by adding the cost of sending such workers home to even higher fines) and continues to pursue a comprehensive interior enforcement policy zealously aimed at unauthorized residents.

[4]When ratified, the Dublin Convention will, among other things, permit its signatories to return asylum applicants to the first EU country in which they arrived. The Schengen Agreement significantly tightens external border controls while eliminating border checks within the Schengen space (see Papademetriou 1996 for a discussion of these agreements).

5

The legislative changes instituted by the Pasqua Law represent a triumph of the Far Right's agenda (and that of the National Front's Jean-Marie Le Pen in particular) over that of France's fragmented political parties.[5] Yet, given France's traditionally open immigration policy—driven by its need for labor, its colonial stretch, and a demographic "deficit" fueled by heavy losses in two world wars and persistently low birth rates—such a change of heart cannot be explained simply by the Right's capacity to seize the reins on an increasingly politicized issue. A broader set of social and economic factors is at play in shaping the politically savvy, though perhaps worrisome, policy responses emerging from the Balladur government.

THE HISTORICAL BACKDROP

The earliest available information on the foreign population in France dates back to its first modern census in 1851.[6] The management of certain aspects of immigration to France, particularly those related to the recruitment of foreigners, began in 1945, with the creation of the National Office for Immigration (ONI)—now called the Office of International Migration (OMI), which falls under the newly renamed Ministry of Integration and Combating Social Exclusion (previously known as the Ministry of Social, Health and Urban Affairs).[7]

The historical record shows that two broad processes have defined French immigration policy. The first involves the absorption

---

[5]Le Pen burst upon the national French political consciousness in the 1983 local elections, after several pro-immigrant socialist initiatives that included a "regularization" program that offered legal permanent resident status to about 140,000 illegally resident foreigners in 1981-82. Wihtol de Wenden (1994:71-74) attributes the organized social activism among ethnic minorities to the granting of freedom of association to foreigners in 1981 and the introduction of a ten-year residence card in 1984.

[6]See Silberman (1992) for an excellent introduction to the methodology and rationale of French immigration statistics.

[7]The OMI is also responsible for recruiting foreign workers (excluding those who enter through bilateral agreements), managing family reunification, and dealing with immigrant health issues. Also within the same Ministry is the Directorate of Population and Migration, which tracks acquisition and loss of French citizenship. The Interior Ministry oversees police and border control functions. Matters of data collection on immigration are under the aegis of the National Institute of Statistics and Economic Studies (INSEE), located within the Ministry of Economy, which publishes the national census—most recently taken in 1990. Finally, the French Office for the Protection of Refugees and Stateless Persons (*Office Français de Protection des Réfugiés et des Apatrides*, or OFPRA) was created in 1954 and falls under the Ministry of Foreign Affairs.

of newcomers from Russia, Poland, Belgium, Italy, Spain, and Portugal. Immigrants from these countries and their descendants continue to have a substantial presence in France, although their numerical significance is declining because of the newer influx from Africa and Asia. According to the 1990 census, of the twelve EU nationalities at that time, the Portuguese comprised the largest foreign (non-citizen) community in France (649,714)—followed by Italians (252,759) and Spaniards (216,047). This compared with, for example, 614,207 Algerians and 572,652 Moroccans (INSEE 1992).

French colonial history explains the second process of French immigration policy: the quest for labor. By the end of World War I, France depended heavily on foreign labor (some from its colonies) to bolster its postwar economy and to assuage national concerns about a shrinking French population.[8] These factors intensified following World War II and through the decolonization period of the late 1950s and early 1960s, when immigrants from the Maghreb, especially Algeria, began to move to the metropole.[9] In 1946, 35,000 Algerians entered France without immigration restrictions. By 1955, the cumulative number of Algerians living in France had reached 200,000 (Garson 1992). The independence of Morocco and Tunisia in 1956, and the signing of the Evian Agreement, which finally brought independence to Algeria in 1962, fed further immigration flows to France, as did some of the special bilateral agreements designed to provide France with a continuous source of labor from individual African countries.[10]

THE POST-1974 PERIOD: THE FICTITIOUS HALT

Although France began to implement immigration control policies in the early 1950s, the relatively free movement of labor continued until July 1974, when France, like all other European

---

[8] For a discussion of "strategic demography" (i.e., linking political goals with population size) and France, see Teitelbaum and Winter 1985.

[9] After Algerian independence in 1962, there was considerable movement to France by both former colonists resident in Algeria and Algerians who had sided with the French during the war of independence.

[10] According to Silverman (1992:43), bilateral agreements "gave an important boost to the numbers of nationals from each country allowed entry into France." In 1963, special agreements were signed with Morocco, Tunisia, Mali, and Mauritania. Senegal and Algeria (through the Franco-Algerian Agreement) became signatories in 1964. Similar agreements with Yugoslavia and Turkey in 1965 continued to usher in a period of growing diversity in French immigration patterns.

Table 1
Foreign Population in Selected European Countries: Total number of foreign-born, percentage of total population, and percentage of foreign population originating in EC[a]
(thousands and percentages)

	1975	1980	1985	1988	1989
Austria	244	283	304	344	387
% of total population		3.7	4.0	4.5	5.1
% of foreign from EC					
Belgium[b]	835	877	847	869	881
% of total population		8.9	8.6	8.8	8.9
% of foreign from EC		8.9	63.6	61.8	61.4
France[c]	3,402	3,714	n.a.	n.a.	n.a.
% of total population	6.6	6.8			
% of foreign from EC	54.3	47.7			
Germany[d]	4,090	4,453	4,379	4,489	4,846
% of total population	6.6	7.2	7.2	7.3	7.7
% of foreign from EC		33.7	31.0	28.4	27.4
Italy[e]	n.a.	299	423	645	490
% of total population		0.5	0.7	1.1	0.9
% of foreign from EC			30.8	25.4	22.8
Netherlands	351	521	553	592	642
% of total population	2.6	3.7	3.8	4.0	4.3
% of foreign from EC	44.2	32.9	29.2	26.5	25.4
Sweden[f]	410	422	389	421	456
% of total population	10	5.1	4.6	5.0	5.3
% of foreign from EC		18.0		15.0	14.5
Switzerland[g]	1,013	893	940	1,007	1,040
% of total population	16.1	14.1	14.5	15.2	15.6
% of foreign from EC		77.1	74.8	72.2	70.9
United Kingdom[h]	2,600	n.a.	1,731	1,821	1,812
% of total population			3.1	3.2	3.2
% of foreign from EC			46.0	48.4	44.3

[a] In this table the terms EC and, as of 1994, EU, apply to the 12 countries of the European Community (Belgium, Denmark, France, Germany, Greece, Ireland, Italy, Luxembourg, The Netherlands, Portugal, Spain, and the United Kingdom) irrespective of the countries' dates of entry into the Community. This designation does not include the three countries—Austria, Finland, and Sweden—whose membership in the Community became effective in 1995.

[b] In 1985, as a result of modifications in the nationality code, some persons who formerly would have been counted as foreigners were included as nationals. This led to a marked decrease in the foreign population.

[c] Population censuses taken in 1975, 1982, and 1990. In this table, data for 1980 reflect those gathered in the 1982 census.

[d] Data up to 1984 and for 1990 are as of September 30; data for 1985-1989 and for 1991 are as of December 31; data for 1994 are as of June 30. Data refer to West Germany up to 1990 and to both East and West Germany from 1991 on.

Table 1, continued

1990	1991	1992	1993	1994	
456	533	623	690	713	**Austria**
5.9	6.8	7.9	8.6	8.9	% of total population
					% of foreign from EC
905	923	909	921	922	**Belgium**
9.1	9.2	9.0	9.1	9.1	% of total population
60.9	60.1		59.6	59.9	% of foreign from EC
3,597	n.a.	n.a.	n.a.	n.a.	**France**
6.3					% of total population
36.5					% of foreign from EC
5,343	5,882	6,496	6,878	6,991	**Germany**
8.4	7.3	8.0	8.5	8.6	% of total population
26.9	25.3	23.2	22.3	22.3	% of foreign from EC
781	897	924	987	899	**Italy**
1.4	1.5	1.6	1.7	1.6	% of total population
16.4	16.2	13.5	15.5	15.3	% of foreign from EC
692	733	757	780	774	**Netherlands**
4.6	4.8	5.0	5.1	5.0	% of total population
24.3	24.0	24.2	24.1	24.9	% of foreign from EC
484	494	499	508	537	**Sweden**
5.6	5.7	5.7	5.8	6.1	% of total population
14.1	13.6	13.3	13.0		% of foreign from EC
1,100	1,163	1,214	1,260	n.a.	**Switzerland**
16.3	17.1	17.6	18.1		% of total population
69.1	66.8	63.3	61.2		% of foreign from EC
1,723	1,750	1,985	2,001	1,946	**United Kingdom**
3.2	3.1	3.5	3.5	3.4	% of total population
42.4	42.3	39.6	36.0	40.7	% of foreign from EC

[e] Data are adjusted to take account of the regularizations that occurred in 1987, 1988, and 1990. The fall in numbers from 1989 results from a review of the foreigners' registers (removing duplicate registrations and accounting for returns).

[f] Some citizens with permits of short duration are not counted (mainly citizens of other Nordic countries).

[g] Numbers of foreigners with annual residence permits (including, up to December 31, 1982, holders of permits of durations less than 12 months) and holders of settlement permits (permanent permits). Seasonal and frontier workers are excluded.

[h] Numbers estimated from the annual Labor Force Survey, prepared by the U.K. Department of Employment.

n.a. = not available

Sources: SOPEMI, *Trends in International Migration* (Paris: Organisation for Economic Co-operation and Development), 1976, 1981, 1993, 1995); and Provisional Country Reports to SOPEMI, 1995.

countries except The Netherlands, called an official if fictive "end"[11] to its temporary labor program. By that time, more than 80 percent of all foreigners coming to France were from North Africa or the Iberian Peninsula, with more than 20 percent each from Portugal and Algeria (Horowitz 1992).

The immediate reason for closing French borders to foreign workers was the changing economic environment, particularly the convulsions following the oil price shock of 1974. Another reason for the change was the entry into the workforce of the "baby boom" generation and the growing participation of women in the labor force. Both of these trends fed an increase in unemployment that has continued almost unabated until the present. According to Tapinos:

> the nature of the interactions between the labor market and immigration has changed profoundly. The new profile of the [indigenous] labor supply—featuring a larger working age population and a higher percentage of women—has substantially cut into the demand for foreign labor, and migration is no longer seen, as it was prior to 1975, as a mechanism to adjust to surplus demand for labor (1995:7).

What is perhaps most important about these movements is that, *despite* the end of the temporary work programs and the shift toward greater immigration controls, France continues officially to consider itself a "country of immigration."[12]

According to the 1990 census, the total foreign (i.e., non-citizen) population legally resident in France was approximately 3.6 million, or 6.3 percent of the population (see Table 1, p. 8).[13] This was a slight reduction from 6.8 percent in 1982 and 6.6 percent in 1975. In 1990, only 36.5 percent of the non-citizen population was from other countries of the European Community, compared with almost 50 percent in the mid-1980s. Conversely, the share of North African immigrants to France rose by nearly 50 percent

---

[11]The so-called end did see a fall in the intake of foreign workers engaged in non-seasonal or other special types of work (see Table 2, p. 12) from approximately 100,000 per year in the early 1970s to about one-tenth that figure ten years later.

[12]One must wonder whether the French public would stand by such a statement as readily today as it has for most of this century.

[13]It is important to note that these figures cannot be compared directly to those for other EU countries, since France does not report statistics on the original nationality of naturalized French citizens. In other words, there are many more persons born outside France or born within France of foreign parents who have subsequently assumed French nationality than the statistics on "foreigners" reveal.

Figure 1
Immigrant Source Regions for Italy, France, and the U.K. in 1993

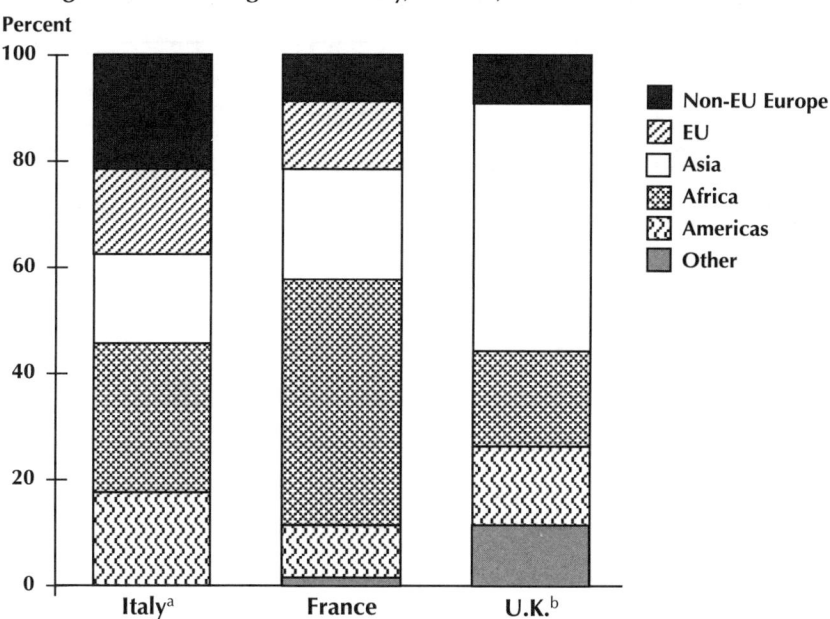

a "Other" = 1 percent.
b "EU" = 0.9 percent.
Source: *Trends in International Migration* (Paris: Organisation for Economic Co-operation and Development [OECD]), 1995.

between 1975 and 1990 (see Figure 1) for the distribution of immigrants in France by region of origin).[14]

THE DILEMMAS OF LABOR IMMIGRATION

France is caught in the classic dilemma that characterizes all immigration regimes. Striving to permit some labor migration demanded by employers while continuing to restrict immigration

---

[14] North Africans comprised 30 percent of permanent admissions to France in 1975; nearly 40 percent through the mid-1980s; and, together with Sub-Saharan Africans, more than 45 percent of the total by 1990 (INSEE 1994:7). This does not, however, imply a consistency in the make-up of the flows. Initially largely comprised of young, single men between the ages of 20 and 35, migration flows since 1974 have, due to family reunification, come to include many more children and a greater proportion of women. Poulain notes two additional changes: the "accentuation" of "the visible face of immigration" and the "ghettoization" of immigrants within certain sections of the West's largest cities, both of which he sees as "the base of the emergence of xenophobic movements" (1994:689-705).

Table 2
Annual Migration to France, by main categories, 1985-1994[a]

	1985	1986	1987	1988	1989
Permanent Workers[c]	9,716	9,867	10,709	12,705	15,592
Temporary Workers[d]	1,243	1,371	1,522	1,889	3,054
Seasonal Workers[e]	86,180	81,670	76,647	70,547	61,868
Family Members[f]	32,545	27,140	26,769	29,345	34,594
Asylum Seekers	28,809	26,196	27,568	34,253	61,372
Total	158,493	146,244	143,215	148,739	176,480

[a] This table documents selective categories of inflows, including permanent settlers and temporary entrants.

[b] 1992 was the first year in which workers from Spain and Portugal had free access to employment anywhere within the European Union (EU). As a result, the number of EU workers peaked in 1992 at 23,768 (out of a total of 42,255).

[c] Includes those workers obtaining a first residence permit valid for at least one year.

[d] Includes those workers holding a (renewable) temporary work permit valid for a maximum of nine months.

in keeping with industrial and other economic and social policy goals, it struggles to reconcile two frequently competing goals.

French law provides for both "temporary" (usually for no more than nine months) and "permanent" (at least one year) labor migration. The government's decision on which type of work permit to issue is based on an assessment of both the employment situation within the profession and the geographic area from which an employer is seeking foreign labor.[15] In addition, the government considers how well the applicant's prospective employer has respected labor regulations in the past and whether or not he or she has maintained equality in wages and working conditions between native and foreign workers.[16] Very few permanent work

---

[15] This criterion is not applied to refugees or in cases of family reunification.

[16] The government also considers whether or not the employer can provide adequate housing for the foreign worker, although this provision is not currently enforced (Moreau 1994). For a discussion of the policies and requirements of key European countries relating to foreign workers seeking to gain admission to engage in a specific task or occupation, see Papademetriou and Yale-Loehr 1996.

Table 2, continued

1990	1991	1992[b]	1993	1994	
22,393	25,607	42,255	24,338	18,349	**Permanent Workers**[c]
3,807	4,075	3,919	4,044	4,063	**Temporary Workers**[d]
58,249	54,241	13,597	11,283	10,339	**Seasonal Workers**[e]
36,949	35,625	32,642	32,408	20,646	**Family Members**[f]
54,813	47,380	28,873	27,564	25,964	**Asylum Seekers**
176,211	166,928	121,286	99,637	79,361	**Total**

[e] Includes those workers holding a work permit valid for a maximum of three months.
[f] Family reunification for foreign nationals already settled in France. Does not include all the families of EU nationals, but only those formally applying to the Office of International Migration for family reunification, a procedure that is not compulsory.
Sources: André Lebon. *Situation de l'immigration et la présence étrangère en France (1993-94).* Paris: *Ministère des Affaires Sociales, de la Santé et de la Ville, Direction de la Population et des Migrations,* December, 1994; and *Ministère de l'integration et de la lutte contre l'exclusion, Direction de la Population et des Migrations,* 1995.

permits are issued to foreigners who do not already have temporary residence or refugee status (see Table 2).[17]

The two-category system of work permits raises questions for the French government not unlike those faced by other labor-importing countries. While the temporary permits allow the government to meet employers' needs, there is concern that once a worker is no longer needed, he or she may continue to work illegally. Furthermore, forcing an immigrant to remain tied to a specific employer and a specific job makes the worker totally dependent on the employer and thus subject to exploitation. However, as Gerard Moreau, Director of the French Population and Migration Directorate, observes, the larger issue "is not how to regulate the entry of migrant workers, but how to organize the national labor market in order to respond to economic needs, now and in the future" (Moreau 1994:13).

---

[17] A third category is composed of seasonal workers, but with a persistently high level of unemployment (hovering at about 12 percent for almost three years), the French government has sharply restricted issuance of seasonal work permits (see Table 2).

An even broader issue is the dichotomy between immigration models that aim at full immigrant integration and those that seek to tie immigration solely to employment—with long-term settlement often an unwanted but tolerated by-product (Tapinos 1995). In the case of France, this dichotomy is somewhat muted, as French immigration policies have developed a hybrid character, not falling at the extremes of either the "settlement" or the "labor" model.[18]

THE CHALLENGE OF UNAUTHORIZED EMPLOYMENT

Intertwined with the inherent tensions between labor needs and social cohesion in France are the linkages between immigration and clandestine work. In fact, governments at both ends of the political spectrum have been increasingly active in regulating the employment of foreigners. The 1974 legislation that attempted to stop all employment-related immigration also contained provisions leading to employer sanctions for hiring illegally resident workers.

Over the past two decades, deterring the employment of unauthorized foreigners by penalizing their employers has gradually become the immigration-control policy of choice of many advanced industrialized societies—and especially of France. Most European countries have seen employer sanctions *first* as a labor-market control measure (i.e., as a tool for checking the spread of the underground economy), *second* as an employment standard (i.e., as a mechanism for preventing unfair labor practices and for controlling the exploitation of "clandestine" migrants), and *only lastly* as a means to control clandestine migration (see Papademetriou 1993a and 1993b). The current preoccupation with controlling illegal immigration, and France's leadership on this issue (and emphasis on interior controls), suggests a reordering of these priorities.

---

[18]However analytically useful ideal constructs such as "settlement" and "labor" migration may be, they are also somewhat misleading. The distinctions are much less precise than intimated, and, over time, policy and administrative decisions lead countries away from some models and toward others. This is especially true as potential immigrants, confronted with stricter controls, turn toward other means, such as tourism, study, asylum applications, and illegal entry, to enter and remain in industrialized countries (see also Papademetriou and Hamilton 1995).

14

France has used employer sanctions for all of these purposes—beginning as early as 1926, then again in 1946, and most recently in 1974. It has been pursuing enhancements and refinements in its "war" against illegal employment with extraordinary zeal along legislative, regulatory, and judicial enforcement paths.[19] Indeed, a major overhaul in 1991 expanded the government's authority to punish employers and their unauthorized workers much more severely.

Part of the strategy relates to the "regularization" of unauthorized immigrants. In 1982, for example, approximately 140,000 workers (out of 150,000 applicants) were granted legal status. As Marie (1994) cautions, however, the focus on "unauthorized" employment has led to the widespread misconception in France that most "illegal jobs"[20] are held by illegal aliens; he points out that there are also "growing numbers of French and legally resident foreign workers whose employment is not in conformity with the law" (1994:120). This recognition of the complexity and the many dimensions of unauthorized employment has significant implications for broader EU policy. The French experience underscores some of the structural characteristics of illegal employment that do not point unequivocally to the immigration status of workers. The fact that citizens, authorized foreign workers, and illegal immigrants are all participating in illegal employment demands a re-examination of the nature of the illegal job market and the socio-economic conditions that keep it going.

NEW DIRECTIONS IN ASYLUM

Like all other EU member countries, France has intensified its border controls and moved firmly toward restricting access to asylum. Most significantly, France, like Germany, has made the

---

[19]Placing the issue of combating the employment of unauthorized immigrants squarely on the EU agenda became one of France's major policy goals during its tenure at the helm of the EU in the first six months of 1995. Typically, agreement proved elusive. Even more typically, however, the strong push on this issue compelled governments that had been reluctant to adopt stronger measures in this regard to reconsider their position. Recent British initiatives in this area, discussed later on in this essay, should be seen partly as a reaction to the discussions concerning the employment of unauthorized immigrants within the EU.

[20]"Illegal" jobs are those outside France's regulatory framework in such areas as pay and work standards or payment of social security contributions; in English, such jobs are more commonly termed "off-the-books," "underground," or "invisible."

Table 3
Asylum Applications in Selected Western European Countries,[a] in thousands, with percentages accepted in parentheses

	1980	1985	1989	1990
Austria	9.3	6.7	21.9	22.8
		(14.5)	(19.0)	(7.0)
Belgium	2.7	5.3	8.1	13.0
			(16.0)	
France	18.8	28.8	61.4	54.8
		(40.0)	(28.1)	(15.7)
Germany	107.8	73.8	121.3	193.1
	(12.0)	(29.2)	(5.0)	(4.4)
Italy	1.5	5.4	2.3	4.7
	(28.6)			(28.0)
The Netherlands		5.6	13.9	21.2
	1.3	(17.4)	(11.7)	(6.6)
Sweden	5.6[c]	14.5	30.0	29.4
			(90.0)	(85.0)
Switzerland	6.1	9.7	24.4	35.8
	(41.9)	(10.0)	(4.9)	(4.9)
United Kingdom	n.a.	4.4	11.6	26.2
		(13.0)	(19.1)	(3.5)

[a] Data do not accurately reflect how many asylum seekers are still in the country. Annual totals can also include persons who have been counted more than once, or who have already left the country. They also may include persons who only stayed a week or so in transit to a third country, as well as persons who left after a few days. Interpretation of the data is further complicated by the fact that some countries include in their tallies the number of principal asylum applicants and their dependents, while others include only the number of principal applicants; for instance, data for Austria and the U.K. refer to principal applicants only, while data for Germany include principal applicants and their dependents.

[b] Data for 1994 are provisional.

[c] This is an approximate figure for individuals granted asylum (including dependents). According to the Swedish Ministry of Labor, in 1980 the total number of persons claiming asylum was not much higher than that of persons granted asylum.

Table 3, continued

1991	1992	1993	1994	
27.3	16.2	4.7	5.1	**Austria**
(12.0)	*(9.8)*		*(13.5)*	
15.4	17.3	26.3	14.3	**Belgium**
(1.6)	*(1.5)*	*(1.1)*		
47.4	28.9	27.6	26.0	**France**
(19.7)	*(29.1)*	*(28.0)*	*(20.0)*	
256.1	438.2	322.8	127.2	**Germany**
(6.9)	*(4.3)*	*(3.2)*	*(7.3)*	
25.5	6.0	1.6	1.8	**Italy**
(4.7)	*(9.8)*	*(8.4)*		
21.6	17.1	35.4	51.9[b]	**The Netherlands**
(6.3)	*(32.6)*	*(23.0)*		
24.4	84.0	37.6	18.6	**Sweden**
(80.0)	*(65.0)*	*(97.0)*		
41.6	18.0	24.7	16.1	**Switzerland**
(3.0)	*(4.5)*	*(13.6)*		
44.8	24.6	22.4	32.8	**United Kingdom**
(1.3)	*(4.5)*	*(7.1)*	*(4.0)*	

Sources: SOPEMI, *Trends in International Migration* (Paris: Organisation for Economic Co-operation and Development), 1981, 1993, and 1995. Provisional Country Reports to SOPEMI, OECD, 1994 and 1995; *World Refugee Survey* (Washington, D.C.: U.S. Committee for Refugees), 1992, 1993, and 1994; *Summary Description of Asylum Procedures in States in Europe, North America and Australia* (Geneva: Secretariat of the Inter-Governmental Consultations on Asylum, Refugees and Migration Policies in Europe, North America and Australia), March 8, 1995; and *Statistical Bulletin*, (London: United Kingdom Home Office, 1995).

necessary legal and constitutional changes to bring its legislation into line with its multilateral agreements with other European countries. For example, France now requires visas for entry into French territory from 158 countries. In addition to entry visas, it demands airport transit visas from nationals of Afghanistan, Albania, Angola, Bangladesh, Eritrea, Ethiopia, Ghana, Haiti, Iraq, Iran, Liberia, Nigeria, Pakistan, Somalia, Sierra Leone, and Zaire[21]—all countries whose nationals are deemed most likely to seek ways to apply for asylum in France. Along with these deterrent measures, France has instituted a 10,000-franc penalty for airlines that transport undocumented asylum seekers (IGC [France] 1994:2).

Despite such increasingly systematic efforts to restrict opportunities for filing asylum claims, a total of 26,044 persons nevertheless applied for asylum in France in 1994. This represented only a slight decrease from the 1993 level of 27,564 applicants (itself a modest drop of approximately 1,300 from the previous year), although it was significantly less than the 47,380 who applied in 1991 and the high of 61,372 in 1989 (see Table 3, p. 16). In 1994, most asylum seekers came from Africa (39 percent), followed by Europe (about 33 percent) and Asia (about 25 percent).[22] Romanians were the largest group (16 percent). Turkey and the former Yugoslavia also produced substantial numbers of asylum seekers (USCR 1995:139).

Since 1990, asylum approval rates have fluctuated, with 20.7 percent of adjudicated cases approved in 1994, 28 percent in 1993, 30 percent in 1992, 20 percent in 1991, and 15.7 in 1990 (USCR 1994:130 and 1995:139).[23] Yet France's approval rate in recent years has been far below the level of the mid-1980s. In 1984, for example, 66 percent of the requests were accepted. And for some nationalities—for example Mauritanians, Zairians, Roma-

---

[21]This is the list of countries as of July 1995, obtained from the Embassy of France, Washington, D.C.

[22]According to the French Ministry of Social, Health, and Urban Affairs, the same set of countries generated about 80 percent of the requests between 1989 and 1992; these countries are Romania, the former Yugoslavia, Angola, Guinea-Conakry, Mali, Mauritania, Zaire, China, India, Pakistan, Sri Lanka, Turkey, Cambodia, Laos, and Vietnam (Lebon 1993:20-21).

[23]Note that France does not have a "safe country" list that would allow it to refuse to hear asylum claims from either the nationals of certain countries or those transiting through those countries. All applications for asylum are thus adjudicated regardless of the country of origin (IGC [France] 1994:10).

nians, Guineans, Algerians, and Malians—the approval rate in 1993 fell well below the overall average of 28 percent (USCR 1994:130). France also retains the right to revoke the ten-year residency permits issued to refugees if OFPRA, in consultation with other ministries, determines that the conditions supporting refugee status according to the 1951 United Nations Convention relating to the Status of Refugees no longer exist.[24]

The situation of former Yugoslavs in France is perhaps indicative of French determination to discourage claimants and restrict access to asylum protection. France has irritated refugee-protection groups, including the U.N. High Commissioner for Refugees (UNHCR), by being among the European countries least receptive to accepting asylum seekers from the former Yugoslavia despite its activism in attempting to resolve the crisis. By mid-1994, only about 15,000 former Yugoslav asylum seekers were estimated to have received asylum in France—far fewer, for example, than those provisionally or permanently resettled in Austria, Germany, or Sweden (see Table 4, p. 20).[25] A government directive issued in August 1992 did, however, lead to greater approval rates for former Yugoslavs seeking temporary protection—"especially those filed by persons formerly resident in areas under the *de facto* control of members of other ethnic groups" (USCR 1994:131). Thus, although the overall asylum approval rate for former Yugoslavs stood at 11.6 percent in 1992, it increased dramatically to 54 percent (and to 82.6 percent for Bosnians) in 1993 (USCR 1994:131).

CITIZENSHIP AND ETHNICITY: *NOS ANCÊTRES LES GAULOIS?*

France has a long history of significant and diverse immigration flows, evidenced by its diverse population base. A recent study by the *Institut National d'Études Démographiques* quantifies this diversity, noting that:

---

[24]Refugee status can be reversed at both the individual and the collective level. "Collective withdrawal" is considered by France in consultation with the U.N. High Commissioner for Refugees when the sending state is believed to have made significant political gains toward democratization (Poland, Hungary, and the Czech and Slovak Republics are examples). Individuals, however, may request special consideration for maintaining their refugee status (IGC [France] 1994:11).

[25]Of these 15,000, about 40 percent had received asylum in the early 1990s, while another 17 percent were registered under programs designed to protect vulnerable groups (USCR 1995:141).

Table 4
Estimated Numbers of "War Refugees" from the Former Yugoslavia in Selected European countries, by status categories, 1994

	Formal Refugee Status[a]	Resettlement under UNHCR auspices	Temporary Protection under UNHCR auspices	Temporary Protection under auspices of host government
Austria	882	n.a.	415	73,000
Denmark	62	n.a.	5,717	12,783[b]
France	>2,000	n.a.	923	n.a.
Germany[c]	14,700	n.a.	3.094	300,000[d]
Italy[e]	26	n.a.	166	n.a.
Sweden	2,509	3,503	n.a.	27,640
Switzerland	3,973	2,714	n.a.	9,601
United Kingdom[f]	25	n.a.	n.a.	n.a.

[a] This category includes those who have been declared Convention refugees, quota refugees, and de facto refugees.

[b] Consideration of the asylum applications of those who have received temporary status has been postponed. The majority of these cases are expected to be adjudicated in 1995 (with permits extended for the duration of the determination process).

[c] It is estimated that, in addition to some 460,000 "war refugees," some 900,000 persons from the former Yugoslavia are lawfully residing in Germany, having arrived there before the outbreak of the conflict, mostly as migrant workers.

[d] Most of these individuals have been granted *Duldung*—a temporary right to remain granted to applicants who have not qualified for asylum but who would nevertheless be endangered if returned to their countries of origin.

the proportion of people born in France with at least a parent or grand-parent who immigrated over the past 100 years is around 20 percent. Among those of foreign origin, 80 percent are French from birth. Thus, immigration has not only actively supported the demography of France, but also has contributed to some important mixing of the population (Tribalat, Garson, et al. 1992:71).

"Early immigration," wrote the Balladur Government's Interior Minister Pasqua, "was essentially a labor policy; the government did not carefully reflect on the non-economic consequences of the massive influx of immigrants" (1994:32-33). One implication of Minister Pasqua's statement is that, despite long-standing immigra-

Table 4, continued

Stay Permits on humanitarian grounds	Asylum Applications pending/no formal status conferred	Estimates of those not registered with authorities	
n.a.	1,259	n.a.	**Austria**
n.a.	n.a.	n.a.	**Denmark**
2,598	5,787	n.a.	**France**
n.a.	n.a.	142,329	**Germany**
83,450	n.a.	10,000	**Italy**
59,402	21,600	n.a.	**Sweden**
31,399	21,600	tens of thousands are estimated to be present without status	**Switzerland**
1,265	n.a.	n.a.	**United Kingdom**[f]

[e] In 1994, Italy issued residence permits to a total of 83,457 former Yugoslavs.
[f] These figures are for 1994 decisions only.
n.a. Indicates that numbers are either unavailable or the category does not exist.
Sources: Some of the figures above are provisional and/or uncertain, and represent our best estimates compiled from the following sources: *World Refugee Survey, 1994* and *World Refugee Survey, 1995* (Washington, D.C.: U.S. Committee for Refugees); "Information Notes on Former Yugoslavia," No. 2/95 (New York: UN High Commissioner for Refugees, Office of the Special Envoy for former Yugoslavia, 1995); *Survey on the Implementation of Temporary Protection* (Humanitarian Issues Working Group of the International Conference on the former Yugoslavia, June 23, 1994; John Salt, *International Migration and the United Kingdom: Report of the U.K. Correspondent to the OECD, 1995* (London: Migration Research Unit, University College London).

tion flows, immigration has never become part of the French nation-building myth in the same way that it has taken root in the American psyche. Weil (1994) attributes this to the difference between being a *country of immigrants,* like the United States, and being a *country of immigration,* like France: In the United States, immigrants retain their roots; in France, although the reliance on immigration is openly acknowledged, official integration efforts and policy statements are geared to denying legitimacy to organized, group-based ethnic differences.

Such diverse postures toward immigration can be attributed largely to fundamentally different concepts of state-citizen relations and the social contract that accompanies the granting of citizenship. France, a strongly secular state, essentially sees the retention of an ethnic identity or "ethnicity" as an obstacle to nation-state solidarity. Opinion polls both document and reinforce this cultural intolerance (see Horowitz 1992:15). As Horowitz has observed:

> The division of the population [in France] into French and foreign implies something that goes to the heart of the differences between France and the United States. The dichotomization of identity means that immigrants who are no longer "foreigners" are presumed to exchange their former identity for a French identity. . . . It is possible to be an Italian in France, but it is not possible to be an Italian-Frenchman in the same way it is possible to be an Italian-American (1992:7).

This is more than semantic hair-splitting. As Simone Veil, Minister of Social, Health, and Urban Affairs in the Balladur Government, argued, "ethnic groups that focus on their own social and cultural lives deprive a nation of an enriching and dynamic vibrancy. Moreover, they frequently curtail the freedom of their members through the opposition to mixed marriages and imposition of alien or illegal customs" (1994:31).[26] Minister Veil's argument directly addresses a set of issues that have become part of the French political landscape since the early 1980s—namely, the success of immigrant groups and their allies in de-linking nationality, citizenship, and voting rights and negotiating what Wihtol de Wenden calls "collective identities" (1994:75). This development has been highly contentious, and reaction to it has led to demands for reaffirming the exclusiveness of French identity. This point of view has found strong support in three influential reports by the *Haut Conseil à l'Integration*—a task force created in 1989 to look at these issues. The *Conseil* was unequivocal in its condemnation

---

[26]Legal rights of immigrant women as defined by French law are one of the concerns of the French Government. To this end, female genital mutilation, polygamy, and other practices that are seen as "contrary to [French] principles" and "unacceptable cultural constraints" to integration have become targets of information and prevention campaigns as well as of new legal penalties. France has also seen an increase in mixed marriages (11.4 percent in 1992 compared to 6.2 percent in 1990) and a decrease in the fertility rate of foreign women to 2.8 percent in 1989-90 compared to 3.2 percent in 1980—and compared to a fertility rate of 1.7 children for French women [FBIS 1994a:29]).

of emphasizing differences and declared that "the logic of equality (among citizens) must prevail over that of (protection and special treatment of) minorities" (quoted in Wihtol de Wenden 1994:76).

Clearly, to most French people, the term "ethnic minority" implies a separate supra-identity beyond the state. In keeping with this perception, they make three primary distinctions among those who are not French by birth. The first, *étranger*, or foreigner, is anyone who is not a French citizen. *Immigré*, a second designation, applies to any resident born outside of France, regardless of nationality. The third term, *français par acquisition*, applies to those who obtain citizenship either through marriage or through birth in France of foreign parents. With growing numbers of French citizens in the latter category, a fourth term, *populations d'origine immigrée*, is becoming more common.

In 1993, 95,500 foreigners assumed French nationality;[27] of these, 73,164 became citizens by declaration or naturalization.[28] Another 22,500—children born in France of foreign parents—became French by making an affirmative declaration, between the ages, of 16 and 21 of their desire to become French citizens (in accordance with Article 44 of the French code, as amended in 1993). In addition, about 15,400 children became French under the provision in Article 23 of the French code,[29] bringing the 1993 total to about 111,000 new French citizens of foreign-born parents (approximately the same as in 1992).[30]

---

[27] This compares with 74,000 naturalizations in 1988; 82,000 in 1989; 88,500 in 1990; 95,500 in 1991; and 95,300 in 1992 (OECD 1995a:225).

[28] Although the number in this category remained quite stable in 1991 (72,213) and 1992 (71,595), it showed an increase from 1989 to 1990, when the figures were 59,508 and 64,976, respectively. The longer-run trend has indeed been one of steady acceleration: The average number of naturalizations by decree and by declaration was 51,719 for the 20 years from 1973 to 1993; 58,973 for the ten years from 1984 to 1993; and 68,291 for the five years from 1989 to 1993 (Lebon 1994:32). France's average naturalization rate from 1988 to 1991 was about 2 percent of the immigrant population, falling toward the lower end of the various rates for other European countries. Austria, for instance, had a rate of 2.8 percent during the same period; Belgium, 0.2 percent; Denmark, 3.4 percent; Germany, 2.7 percent; the U.K., 3.4 percent; and Sweden, 5.4 percent (OECD 1994a:50).

[29] Under Article 23, children born to an Algerian parent before independence, or to a parent who resided in one of the French colonies before independence, are entitled to French citizenship.

[30] The citizenship category is particularly interesting in France from a statistical point of view. With naturalization, substantial numbers of immigrants each year statistically disappear as "foreigners" and become French citizens. This in large part explains the relative stability in the number of foreigners in France over the last 10 to 15 years (see also *supra* fn. 13).

Africans made up the majority of new citizens in 1993. *Maghrebins* accounted for 44 percent of the total, with those from the rest of Africa adding another 12 percent.[31] Indeed, by 1990, Africa had already surpassed Europe (excluding the European Newly Independent States of the former Soviet Union) as the principal source of new French citizens. In 1993, Moroccans led the list of newly naturalized citizens, followed by Algerians,[32] Tunisians, Portuguese, and Cambodians (Lebon 1994). According to the Ministry of Social, Health, and Urban Affairs, roughly 68 percent of all new French citizens come from the former colonial empire and from Francophone countries (Decouflé and Tetaud 1993).

IMMIGRATION, CULTURAL DISTANCE, AND ISLAM

In the French immigration scenario, it is worth exploring in some depth the heightened tensions that are emerging specifically in relation to the triad of immigration, the state, and Islam—the second largest religion in France. In a sense, France is caught between Descartes and the Koran, and it is this dilemma that undergirds some of France's greatest immigration challenges.

Much of the current political debate in France is fueled by a popular perception that the increasingly "visible" immigrant Muslim minority is posing a direct challenge to state tenets of secularity. This is particularly problematic for a country like France, where, since the early part of this century—a relatively short period of time in comparison with most other aspects of the French citizen-state relationship—religion has been expected to be an extremely private and discreet issue.[33] Fear of "Africanization" or "Islamization," accompanied by related intense concerns about internal security and terrorism (most prominently associated with the ongoing political struggle in Algeria), underlie most of the restrictive legislative and governmental measures on immigration of recent years.

---

[31]This proportion does not include 22,500 minors who were naturalized—or who, prior to the change in the French nationality code, acquired French nationality automatically at the age of 18 (Lebon 1994:34).

[32]Large-scale Algerian naturalizations are a relatively new phenomenon and a rational response to anti-North African sentiment in France.

[33]As Tapinos argues, "there can be no integration if, for example, Islam in Europe cannot adjust to being a religion that is practiced in private" (1995:15). This remains true despite (a) the increasing convergence in labor market participation rates for women, unemployment, and fertility levels between French and immigrants, and (b) the increase in mixed marriages.

THE RISE OF ANTI-IMMIGRANT FORCES IN FRENCH POLITICS

The National Front's assault on immigration has continued unabated. During the 1995 presidential campaign, it called for sending immigrants home as its prescription for eliminating the French unemployment problem. Le Pen received 15 percent of the first round vote—his highest result in 30 years (*New York Times* 1995b:53). More telling, however, was the National Front's performance during the June 1995 municipal elections. Exploiting the government's vulnerability on unemployment, crime, and official corruption, and linking those issues to its standard anti-immigrant fare, the National Front polled over 30 percent of the vote in the first round, including 43 percent in Vitrolles, a suburb of Marseilles (*The Economist* 1995e:53). The post–first round political maneuvering meant that only three National Front mayors were finally elected in the second round—but in important constituencies: Toulon (France's fifteenth largest city, with a population of 170,000); Marignane (population 33,000); and Orange (population 28,000)—all near the Mediterranean. (In addition, Nice, France's fifth largest city, with a population of 346,000, elected a former National Front militant as its mayor.)

Following the elections, the Front's mayors announced that they would implement "national preference" policies in housing, jobs, education, and welfare. Although such initiatives would be of dubious legality under current law, the systematic devolution of authority to localities during the last two decades means that mayors have considerably more autonomy on many of these matters than is generally appreciated (*The Economist* 1995f:48-52). In any event, "national preferences," even if only partially feasible under current law, mark a further deterioration of the immigration debate in France and are likely to lead both to some "accommodation" by the French government and to a certain amount of replication by anti-immigrant movements in Europe and elsewhere.

One of the clearest examples of popular ambivalence about Islam and immigration is reflected in the ongoing debate about Islamic headscarves. In 1989, three young girls refused to remove their headscarves in school. Their refusal was seen as a public challenge to French efforts at integration and a rejection of secular public schools. The event did much more than reveal what Hoffmann (1993:67) calls the "French penchant for turning small incidents into grand symbolic issues." It crystallized a whole series of debates as well as national soul-searching about France's newest immigrants—North African and, to a lesser extent, Sub-Saharan African immigrants. These newcomers are seen as emanating from points of great cultural distance, as manifested in such private and public behaviors as polygamy, religious clothing and practices, and attitudes toward women's rights.

In 1989, the government initially allowed the authorities at each French school to make their own decisions relating to proper attire. By 1994, however, the government had reversed itself and was strongly discouraging[34] the wearing of Islamic headscarves, contending that the headscarf "divid[ed] Muslims and non-Muslims" (*New York Times* 1994:4). This official reversal was largely a political response to the resonance of the Far Right's anti-immigrant message. The success of Le Pen's National Front in the first round of the presidential elections and the subsequent municipal elections in mid-1995, and growing concerns across the continent about the influx of immigrants from the South and East, made it virtually impossible to continue to leave the management of the headscarf affair to the local level.

EDUCATION AND IMMIGRATION

More fundamentally, however, the headscarf incident illustrates the heightened political role of the public school as an ideological battlefield on the issues of the integration of immigrants and long-term French social and cultural cohesion. Education, according to Boyzon-Fradet (1992:161), has taken on a new, more political character since the mid-1960s. She argues that:

> fundamental changes in the migratory phenomenon and especially the birth of most immigrant children in France, but

---

[34]Attempts to "prohibit" the practice were struck down by the *Conseil d'État*.

also and above all the political debate stimulated by the right and far-right parties, have led the Minister of National Education . . . to clearly affirm the goal of giving absolute priority to the integration of immigrant children into the standard school system and, more recently, of integrating education policy into an overall immigration policy.

Boyzon-Fradet's assertion is very much in line with one of the reports issued by the already-mentioned *Haut Conseil à l'Integration*. In examining and coordinating the government's "policy relating to the integration of immigrant residents or those of immigrant origin," the *Conseil* noted the weakening of the traditional institutions of integration, such as the army and unions in France (Tribalat, Garson, et al. 1991:114).

A similar attitude was evident in the findings of the Presidential Commission on Nationality. Following numerous interviews and an extensive program of research, the so-called Long Commission emphasized the increased importance of the school as the locus of fundamental integration activities. According to the Commission (1988:28):

> This weakening of institutions and of universalist values around which the national tradition has been elaborated and which have permitted the integration of foreign populations over the last two centuries constitutes a veritable danger for the future of the nation.

French concern about the role of the school in building and maintaining a "nation" is acute. Other countries—for example Belgium, Denmark, Sweden, and the U.K.—have allowed some of their immigrants "to opt out of the culture of the receiving country" by permitting separate state-supported schools (Coleman 1993:338). in contrast, the headscarf case exemplifies the French insistence on inculcating immigrants across-the-board with Western values and norms.[35]

---

[35]Coleman discusses what are perceived as "problem areas of integration" for European immigrants and calls education "a key component" in this process (1993:336).

THE STATE RESPONDS: AMBIVALENCE AND MISUNDERSTANDING

The nation-state is not only a fact; it is also "an idea or an ideal—a way of thinking about political and social membership" (Brubaker 1989:3). The French state clearly views any promotion of a separate community identity in the public sphere as an obstacle to nation-state solidarity. Thus, inward-looking tendencies by communities divided along national and/or ethnic lines are perceived as fundamental threats to social cohesion.

Islam adds another dimension to this issue. In secular states, perceptions of religious display may and often do take on a political dimension. Such displays can assume both a political and a religious/cultural identity by pushing the boundaries of secularity and by blurring the lines of public and private domains.

The French state's actions reveal a deep discomfort about Islam and go to the heart of French preoccupations with cultural identity and secularity. The state's hesitancy and vacillation during the headscarf affair and its aftermath attest to a national ambivalence about whether a "benign Islam"[36] can indeed exist in France. This ambivalence is obvious in the thinking of Jean-Claude Barreau, principal advisor to former Minister of Interior Pasqua. Barreau believes that France can overcome the challenges of Islam *only* if the state does not make any more concessions for the Islamic community than for other communities.[37]

The state's strategy of denying public space to what is perceived as religious particularism results from a widespread conception of a monolithic Islam that also permeates official French attitudes toward the Islamic world in general. The equation "immigrant worker = *Maghrebin* = Arab = Muslim = fundamentalist," along the lines of "Iranian = fanatic and terrorist" has the effect of reducing Islam to a single malevolent force, and hence to its lowest, most-feared denominator (Taguieff 1991:189-193). This pro-

---

[36]"Benign" in this sense refers to an Islam that is not "ostentatious" and public, is respectful of women's rights as understood within French legal culture, and does not challenge the supremacy of the state in the public sphere.

[37]Interview with Kimberly Hamilton, July 1, 1994. Barreau, former director of OMI, has been under attack by the Left, especially for his publication *On Islam in General and on the Modern World in Particular*, in which he writes that Muslims could integrate into French society only if they relinquished "archaic Muslim practices" (*New York Times* 1991:3).

cess, which Cesari (1994) has called *"totalisation,"* becomes the foundation of a political strategy that allows the state to move nearly seamlessly from a particular incident, such as the headscarf affair, to concerns about a unified fundamentalist attack by Muslim immigrants on the secular French state. Such a strategy ignores the differences among various immigrants, and especially among new generations of children of Muslim parents who will grow up in France. It also denies the possibility of finding any accommodation between the public practice of Islamic religion and the state, along the lines of that between the state and the Jewish community in France.

INTERNAL AND EXTERNAL DIMENSIONS

Islam, and its perceived challenge to France, has both an internal political dimension and an external geopolitical one. On the domestic front, by defining the boundaries of secularity in very narrow terms, France is seeking to reinforce its traditional requirement that immigrants comply with exacting standards for residence, citizenship, and integration in France. This has had two effects. First, it has exacerbated—at least in the short term—an "us" and "them" mentality. While these strict boundaries are likely to blur over time (and certainly over generations), there remains the needling challenge of how best to overcome the "tension between citizenship and social exclusion" (Weil and Crowley 1994:123).

Second, such a policy inflates the value of the French *nation* in contradistinction to French *nationality*. Although immigrants may eventually become citizens, government rhetoric and policies send the unmistakable message that—despite having become citizens, participated in French military commitments, and shared their adopted country's history and language—immigrants will be denied an equal hold on the nation. Because of certain cultural attributes, construed by the state as "particular," they will remain, by definition, "outsiders."

Domestic reaction and policy relate, in large part, to the geopolitical concerns of the state. France's increasingly tough stance on Islam reflects its preoccupation with two interrelated concerns on which it seems to have both diminishing control and a reduced ability to influence the views and behavior of its allies. The first is continuing instability in Algeria, which spilled over into

French territory for the first time with the December 1994 hijacking in Algiers of an Air France plane (eventually stormed by French troops in Marseilles) and, since then, with a wave of bombings that has frayed the nerves of both the authorities and the public. Even before the hijacking, in April 1994, a joint French-Algerian working group had amended a 1960s agreement regulating the entry and residence of Algerians in France. The new provisions require an "extended visa" of all Algerians planning to stay in France more than three months and place some restrictions on family and other visits. Furthermore, Algerians wishing to visit France for less than three months must now have a return ticket as well as proof of financial means sufficient to maintain themselves for the duration of their stay. The French government also reserves the right to deport illegal immigrants *presumed* to be Algerians, even in the absence of official documentation of Algerian citizenship (FBIS 1994b:22).[38] Algeria is a sobering reminder that even the most mature immigration relationships can be adversely affected by concerns that civil upheaval in one country will lead to immigration consequences for the other country.

The second and related concern is the spread of fundamentalist Islam within France. By clamping down on public displays of Islam, the state signals to its partners in foreign affairs that it will remain tough on Islamic fundamentalism, a growing Western concern. This is especially meaningful in the aftermath of the World Trade Center bombing in New York and various other acts that have been associated with fundamentalist Islam. Some of France's partners, however, and particularly the United States, argue that such a posture may have damaging long-term consequences. They suggest that treating Islam as a monolith, in addition to being misguided, denies opportunities for developing or strengthening relationships with moderate Islamic states and moderate voices within Islamic states.

Critics of French policy argue further that it is necessary to create the conditions for being French and Muslim at the same time. As with other religions, a secular Islam already exists—one

---

[38]According to the French Organization of Immigrant Workers Information and Support Group (GISTI), this provision was contained in a draft agreement signed in April 1994 by the Algerian and French governments—which remained confidential until November 1994. GISTI has criticized this as being "criminal" in light of the Algerian political situation (FBIS 1994b:22).

that respects and practices religious rituals while remaining fully French. As Wihtol de Wenden (1993:177) writes, ". . . Europe is an opportunity for Islam: it offers the chance to confront modernity, secularity, democracy, and the equality of rights between men and women."

In addition, secular space in France is in no way "neutral"; it is filled with contested meaning. As Dalil Boubakeur, rector of the Paris mosque, noted in the wake of recent events in Algeria, the atmosphere surrounding immigrants and French society is balanced at a "fragile consensus" (*Financial Times* 1994b:3). Similarly, Noiriel (1992:75) has suggested that:

> French intellectuals are incapable of thinking of assimilation other than in terms of "ethnic compatibility" (what is now called "cultural distance"). . . . [T]he *leitmotif* of French political thought on immigration was that in order to preserve the identity of the French people, a policy of ethnic selection must be applied. However, it was impossible to do so officially without publicly contradicting the fundamental principles of the Republic that are fixed in republican law.

Living with contradiction is not uncommon. For France, the Muslim dimension of its immigrant community has clearly complicated the challenge. This is especially true given the broader international implications—real or perceived—of Islam for the West.

Ultimately, it is unlikely that Islam and immigration will diminish as factors influencing French domestic politics and French relations with the southern Mediterranean basin. These defining issues will be permanent fixtures of the French political and cultural landscape. The continuing tension therefore should not be underestimated. The French nightmare is that aid to the Algerian government might not be sufficient to prevent a political upheaval that could lead to a mass exodus. Such an exodus, in addition to spilling over and destabilizing Algeria's neighbors, would likely create nothing less than an "immigration emergency" in France (as fleeing Algerians with or without the right to French domicile nonetheless sought to enter France) and would further intensify French wariness toward its immigrant communities of Islamic faith.

UNDERSTANDING THE DEBATE

Political and economic conditions in France make for a political tinderbox. The combustible materials include a debilitating economic recession, an unemployment rate that climbed quickly and has hovered stubbornly at about 12 percent,[39] a political reversal of extraordinary magnitude in the 1993 elections (when the conservatives trounced the ruling socialists), difficulties over the referendum on ratification of the Maastricht Treaty creating the European Union (which was approved by the slimmest of margins),[40] and the terrorist campaigns of 1995. Such complicated passions often lead to simplistic solutions. This became plainly obvious both in the rancorous debate leading up to the passage of the 1993 immigration control law[41] and the role that immigration and anti-government rhetoric played in the 1995 electoral campaigns discussed earlier.

The French government's continuing goal in its immigration initiatives is not just to respond to the domestic political debate, but to move toward coordination with the European Union in terms of the elimination of internal borders, the adoption of stricter labor-market controls, and the coordination of broader political and economic activities with regard to immigration. French conservatives, both Jacques Chirac's RPR (Rally for the Republic) and the UDF (French Democratic Union), believe that these measures would provide effective control of illegal immigration, curb abuses in obtaining French citizenship or refugee status, and speed the

---

[39]In 1993, French output fell by 1 percent—the deepest recession in France since World War II. In 1994, output rose by 2.6 percent, with growth expected to be in the 3.5 to 4.0 percent range in 1995. The stubbornness of the unemployment rate is extremely troubling. Underlying it is the same set of fundamentals in evidence in many other advanced industrial economies. Among them are tax, regulatory, and fiscal government policies that reduce the competitiveness of French products; negative perceptions about the quality of French products; inefficient production processes; and deficiencies in the training of the French workforce. France is not yet competitive enough in the international arena to be able to create enough high-wage jobs to bring its unemployment rate down significantly. It must, for instance, create 150,000 net new jobs per year just to stay even with the number of new job seekers (see *The Economist* 1995c:42).

[40]The domestic ramifications of and negative popular reactions to Maastricht are far from over and attest to the democratic deficit predicament that the French government has created for itself.

[41]The government credits this law with the 30 percent drop in immigration—almost entirely in family reunification—in 1994.

expulsion of illegally resident foreigners.[42] From the other major political perspective (that of the Socialist and Communist parties), however, such initiatives are seen broadly as an attempt to subvert the fundamental principle of universal human rights on which the French Republic was founded—or at the very least as a placating "tip of the hat" to the Far Right. From a third perspective, immigrant and human rights organizations together with church groups and other advocacy associations view the legislation as a racially motivated attack on France's immigrant communities.

A final dimension of French responses to immigration relates to France's presidency of the expanded fifteen-member European Union during the first half of 1995. French leadership has been accompanied by the re-emergence of substantive EU interest in the southern and eastern Mediterranean (after a period in which concern with Central and Eastern Europe was dominant); the new pattern was continued by the Spanish presidency in the second half of 1995 and is certain to become even more central during the Italian turn at the EU presidency in the first half of 1996.[43] France has succeeded in shoring up Algeria's financial status through agreements with the International Monetary Fund and the Paris Club. In addition, the EU agreed to invest $6.1 billion toward economic reforms, primarily in the Mediterranean region (FBIS 1995:1).

The French immigration drama can be read, at least to a certain extent, as the penetration of French political space by the European Union's priorities. It should be emphasized again, for instance, that the French have made the necessary constitutional

---

[42] On January 5, 1994, then Interior Minister Pasqua announced the creation of a new government agency called the *Direction Centrale du Contrôle de l'Immigration et de la Lutte Contre l'Emploi des Clandestins* (DICCILEC) to track down unauthorized foreigners. The DICCILEC became operational after a government decree was passed on October 16, 1994. (The Juppé government adheres to the principles behind this initiative with equal rigor.) Pasqua has admitted, however, that force alone will not mitigate unauthorized immigration and has emphasized the need for foreign aid to bolster the faltering economies of sending countries (*Service d'Information et de Diffusion du Premier Ministre* 1994:23).

[43] This has been more of a balancing effort than an abandonment of Eastern Europe. The "Balladur Pact," a French strategy to promote EU security, links EU cooperation with its eastern neighbors to respect for border integrity and minority rights. While this flows almost directly from the Balkan situation, the linkages to migration are clear. *The Economist* (1995a:46) described the "Balladur Pact" as one "in which EU friendship for the countries of Eastern Europe will depend on their willingness to respect the [West's] frontiers and the rights of their ethnic minorities."

FRENCH DOMESTIC POLITICS AND ECONOMIC AND MONETARY UNION (EMU)

At the end of 1995, French public-sector strikes paralyzed France. The strikes were called in response to proposed austerity measures designed to bring the French public- sector deficit under 3 percent of gross domestic product (GDP) within two years, partly by reducing social security benefits. The size of the proposed reductions would appear marginal in most other countries that have had to confront the limits of their welfare state. Not so for France's public employees, however, who took to the streets in massive numbers to protest modest changes in their health care and retirement systems as well as deeper reforms in public-sector union control over certain aspects of the enormous public health fund and subsidies for certain public services—particularly the deficit-ridden rail system.

Neither the merits of the government's actions (which are strong and long overdue) nor the Juppé government's political clumsiness (the reforms were announced after several false starts at economic "reform" during the government's first six months in office and following an extraordinary waste of political capital on such issues as nuclear testing) dispel the suspicion that the austerity measures were tied to the wrong policy goal. The proper goal would have been to acknowledge that France can no longer afford the social entitlements that the French people in general (and the French public servants in particular, who, unlike their private-sector counter-

changes to comply with the spirit of Maastricht. The continuing process of European integration is not, however, solely responsible for forcing the National Assembly's hand. Other influences, such as the perception of job competition with immigrants, security threats, and the growth in ethnic enclaves—with their attendant implications for societal cohesion—have combined with popular demands and local headline-grabbing events to bring increased parts, were until now protected from cuts in their benefits) have come to expect and to which they are strongly attached. In a competitive global economy, the financing of such entitlements is generally unsustainable. Instead, the government chose to tie the need for its austerity package to the importance of French leadership within the EU and, more specifically, to French entry into the EU's Economic and Monetary Union (EMU) as a founding member in 1999.

Entry into the EMU requires meeting certain criteria of "economic convergence." In addition to exchange-rate stability, inflation-rate benchmarks, and a total government debt that does not exceed 60 percent of GDP (which the French can meet), membership also requires an annual public deficit of no more than 3 percent of GDP for two consecutive years. France's public deficit was 6 percent in 1994 and is projected to be 5 percent in 1995.

Although perhaps worthwhile, charter membership in the EMU is clearly a goal that does not resonate well with the many French who have now made the EMU yet another target—in addition to immigrants, international trade accords and, underlying both, an unresponsive government—for their fears about economic security and their frustration with forces over which they seem to have less and less control. (*The Economist*, 1995h:11-12; 1995j:19-21; and 1995k:49-50.)

pressure on the French government for intervention in the field of immigration policy.

Some have argued that the changes in French legislation regarding immigration, along with anti-immigrant comments from various political leaders, are merely masterful posturing to deny the Far Right the political space to carry out its own electoral agenda. The ability of the mainstream presidential candidates to keep immigration largely off the table during the May 1995 presidential campaign lends support to this interpretation. According to this line of thought, the changes in legislation need not pose a serious threat to the protection of immigrants or to the maintenance of refugee rights—a proposition that is far less sustainable.

It is also tempting to construe the immigration debate as one that pits the state's concerns about security against individual immigrant and refugee needs for rights and protection—economic, cultural, and political. Such zero-sum logic plays readily into nativist fears and leads to endless searches for border and interior enforcement solutions to the migration challenge. At the extreme, it also places the state in opposition to any individual who is viewed as an outsider, regardless of his or her contributions to the national well-being—thus undermining the very foundations of governmental legitimacy in a democratic framework.

No doubt France will continue, within the EU, to focus on the challenges of South-to-North immigration, both in the context of its domestic politics (for which the preoccupation with unwanted immigration from the Maghreb is paramount) and in the context of its ambitions to continue to play a dominant role in shaping the future of the EU. But the two directions are not always compatible, particularly as policy and political priorities shift. For instance, while France has succeeded in making its priorities about illegal immigration controls and aid to the Maghreb countries into principal EU policy themes, it has had to backtrack on a policy goal that had been a French priority since the mid-1980s (but that clearly is a lesser one in the past couple of years): a Europe free of internal frontiers. France had been pursuing that goal both within a smaller subgroup of core EU member states (the "Schengen group") and in the larger context of the full Union. Early in 1995, some of the Schengen countries (primarily France, Germany, and the Benelux countries) agreed to implement the elimination of *internal* border controls on an experimental basis by transferring adequate resources to a stringent system of *external* border controls (i.e., controls at the point of entry into Schengen space). Soon after the provisional implementation of the accord, however, heightened concern about the ability of the new measures to protect effectively against drug-traffickers and terrorists led France to abandon many of the accord's provisions and to obtain an additional six-month extention before the accord becomes fully operational.

France's moves must be watched with care as it struggles to reinforce the bond between the state and the individual partly by devising more effective unilateral and multilateral immigration controls. As France pursues its complex domestic and regional agenda, immigrants and asylum seekers can easily become pawns in the two more profound struggles: maintaining social cohesion in the midst of a fundamental questioning of the meaning of full social and political membership, and shoring up France's place in a supranational Europe whose whole still has an opportunity to be much larger than the sum of its parts. Neither challenge is likely to be resolved before the turn of the century.

3. ITALY: COMING TO TERMS WITH "RECEIVING" COUNTRY STATUS

While France's responses to the deteriorating politics surrounding immigration and asylum issues have been dramatic, events in Italy have been nothing short of a political revolution. The revelation of decades of corruption involving key members of the country's political and corporate elites led to the disintegration of the Christian Democrats and their Socialist coalition partners in the March 1994 general elections. The subsequent struggle for influence and power by a variety of grassroots and opposition parties—and the ignominious collapse of conservative Prime Minister Silvio Berlusconi's *Forza Italia* government in December 1994—have left analysts wondering just what kind of phoenix will rise from the ashes.

Coming to terms with the profound—and ongoing—political changes in Italy has displaced immigration from the top of the policy agenda. In many ways, however, immigration remains a visible and intermittently volatile political issue. For instance, gains made initially in municipal and later in national elections by the Democratic Party of the Left (PDS—formerly the Communist Party), the neofascist Italian Social Movement (MSI),[44] and, most pertinent for this discussion, the populist Northern League, hold significant implications for the politics and atmosphere surrounding immigration policy.[45] This is

---

[44] In January 1994, the MSI changed its name to the National Alliance.

[45] The Northern League, supported by the wealthy industrial regions of the North, has built its appeal and policies on a platform dedicated to protest "against rule by a corrupt Rome, against immigration, and against the transfer to the undeserving [Italian] south... of wealth created in the [Italian] north" (*The Economist* 1993:9). Partly as a result of their anti-immigrant platforms, both the Northern League and the MSI (which until recently had taken a lower-key approach to exploiting xenophobia) captured a significant number of votes in the November and December 1993 municipal elections in four of Italy's major cities: Rome, Naples, Genoa, and Venice.

especially true given the Italian elites' political epiphany that their country's future will be shaped by immigration, not emigration,[46] as had been the case historically.

Italians first became aware of this shift in the direction of migration flows after the oil price shock of the mid-1970s. A 1978 study by *Censis* settled on a rough estimate of about 450,000 immigrants in Italy (see Collicelli 1995:143). It was not until the 1980s, however, that the country began to feel the impact of truly significant numbers of immigrants. In 1985, Italy's foreign population was estimated at approximately 423,000. By 1991, that number had more than doubled, reaching 896,800 (OECD 1995a:194). In another indication of the newness of the flow, a 1991 *Censis* study found that 58.1 percent of the immigrants it interviewed had been in Italy for less than three years (see Collicelli 1995:144).[47] By 1994, the official foreign population estimate had increased only slightly, to 899,100. However, this figure referred only to those who held legal residence permits (OECD 1994b:17). In 1994, according to most estimates, about 1.5 million foreigners—both legal and unauthorized[48]—were thought to be working in Italy, a country of 57 million people. Moroccans represented the largest group, numbering 92,617, followed by former Yugoslavs (89,444) and Americans (56,714) (OECD 1995b:2, 20).

Agriculture (particularly but no longer almost exclusively in southern Italy), the tourist industry, the fishing industry, the household and personal services industry, and street vending are sectors with the highest concentrations of Third World immigrants. Increasingly, however, such immigrants are spreading throughout Italy's vast hidden economy and are even making inroads into a variety of more formal but less desirable (in terms of both social

---

[46]The fact that Italian emigration to the United States is nonetheless continuing, although at low rates, and that Italians continue to be among the two leading nationalities of illegal immigrants in New York (the other being the Irish; see INS 1995:Table 4), presumably gives pause to some Italians about how they should treat those foreigners in their midst who are in an illegal status.

[47]After 1991, the number of foreigners holding residency permits declined somewhat, while the number of new entries leveled off. This is thought to be due both to the Italian labor market's limited capacity to absorb newcomers and to the restrictive effects of Italy's 1990 immigration law (OECD 1994a:81-82).

[48]By late in 1995, when the immigration control issue received one of its periodic politically inspired "boosts," estimates of the unauthorized immigrant population ranged between 300,000 and 1 million. Most responsible analysts acknowledge that there are at least 500,000 illegal immigrants in Italy (see *Financial Times* 1995:2).

standing and wages) economic activities, such as tanning, steel, ceramics, and the more mechanized agribusiness in Northern Italy (see Barsotti and Lecchini 1994).[49]

Despite a growing concern about immigration throughout the 1980s, and a serious attempt in the late 1980s to regularize the status of illegal immigrants through two rolling amnesty programs, it was not until 1990 that the Italian government moved immigration control toward the center of its policy agenda. The Italian strategy had two components that it implemented in tandem: a domestic one that involved the passage of the Martelli Law, the first "comprehensive" Italian immigration legislation ever, and an international one, aimed at making the response to unwanted immigration an important item on the multilateral agenda.[50]

However, it was the Albanian refugee crisis of 1991—when approximately 40,000 Albanian asylum seekers crossed the Adriatic in two successive waves—that forced a conscious about-face in Italy's generally low-key approach to immigration policy.[51] Although most of the Albanians from the March exodus were allowed to stay, Italy repatriated almost all of the Albanians who arrived in August. This second wave was followed by intense negotiations between Rome and Tirana to secure Albania's promise to prevent further mass flights and to assist with returnees—in essence turning Albania from a "sending" to a "safe" country in the course of less than one year.

The Albanian crisis caught Italy completely unprepared; its resolution temporarily tarnished the country's standing both with international organizations, such as the UNHCR, and with interna-

---

[49]Between 1992 and 1993, for instance, the total number of foreigners present in Italy grew by 10.8 percent in the north, by 6.8 percent in the center (close to the national average), and by only 1 percent in the south; in the islands, there was a decline of 9.7 percent (OECD 1994b:2).

[50]In fact, in two feverish years (from early in 1990 to mid-1992) Italian pressure to force immigration onto the multilateral agenda was nothing less than extraordinary. In addition to holding a well-received international conference in Rome, followed by an even more remarkable (for the mere fact that it took place, rather than because of any results it achieved) ministerial meeting, Italians became extremely active in the European Community and the OECD and even became motive forces in placing immigration on the final communique of the 1991 Group of Seven (G-7) meeting held in Houston, Texas.

[51]Official Italian estimates put the March influx at 21,300 and the August one at 17,000. U.S. State Department reports cite as many as 28,000 and 20,000, respectively.

tional public opinion.[52] The public and official outcry following the chaotic scenes of Albanian "boat people" in the Italian port of Bari, their subsequent containment in a soccer stadium, and their eventual repatriation were partly responsible for Italy's determined search for multilateral solutions and responses to migration challenges.

Simultaneously, however, Italy has moved forward in fits and starts to establish a responsive immigration policy apparatus, including policies to address the root causes of flight. For instance, Italy established a bilateral aid program for Albania, which delivered approximately $150 million in grants and credits between 1992 and 1995.[53] More important, Italy persuaded the EU to commit substantial "European" resources to Albania, thus effecting the *de facto* "burden-sharing" that had eluded Germany until mid-1995. In that year, the EU made simultaneous five-year commitments of 6.7 billion European currency units (Ecus) (US$8.7 billion) for Eastern Europe and 4.7 billion Ecus (US$6.1 billion) for the Mediterranean region at the Cannes Summit in June (FBIS 1995:1).

Italy's perspective and concerns with respect to immigration are in many ways similar to those of Germany, another sudden immigration "front-line" state, although Italy's focus is on South-to-North rather than East-to-West migration. Its own front-line status has led Italy to try since 1991 to promote systematic efforts to address the causes of Third World migration through initiatives that would commit the EU to sustained development assistance, broadly defined, to regions of high emigration. Supported by several other European countries—especially France and other Mediterranean EU member states, but also Switzerland and the Nordic countries (who are equally concerned about unauthorized migration and fraudulent asylum claims from the South)—Italy has

---

[52]What constitutes a politically "acceptable" response to unwanted mass immigration has changed considerably since 1991—to some degree perhaps as a result of the muted reaction of the international community to Italy's action. In any event, in 1996, the Italian response would evoke much less of a reaction either within or outside of Italy. In most quarters, Italy might now even be praised for its "strong" and unequivocal response. See Papademetriou and Hamilton 1995, for a discussion of these issues.

[53]This ongoing engagement has also allowed Italy to prevail upon Albania to require visas from Asians, who had begun to use Albania as a launching pad to Italy and the rest of Europe.

been preaching the gospel of "burden-sharing" in as many fora as it can influence. Its goal has been to press on these bodies the case for coordinated, systematic actions on issues related to population growth, economic development, and refugee-generating political, ethnic, and religious conflicts.

Italy's intense interest in persuading the other advanced European industrial democracies to commit to a course of coordinated and persistent attention to the root causes of unwanted immigration is unlikely to wane. The issue is of continuing political importance, particularly in light of Italy's volatile domestic situation and the ease with which immigration issues can be exploited by both ends of the political spectrum for electoral gain. The continuing influx of unauthorized immigrants from Africa, together with alarmingly growing seepages from Albania and the former Yugoslavia, mean that the issue is never too far from the public eye.

The political volatility of the issue and the complex ways in which it cuts across the Italian political spectrum again emerged in full display in the second half of 1995 in efforts to breathe life into and once again consolidate the immigration control agenda.[54] That agenda had been sidelined since 1992 as a result of the country's understandable preoccupation with the most fundamental crisis of the legitimacy of its political institutions since the end of the Second World War. The revival of that agenda—and the return of immigration to center stage in Italian politics[55]—came about when a parliamentary commission exploring the issue reported out a provisional text of a bill with the help of the votes of both the National Alliance and the Northern League (which are bitter rivals on virtually all other issues) and over the strenuous objections of the Party of the Democratic Left (PDS), which, together with the Northern League, has been a principal backer of Lamberto Dini's government of technocrats.[56]

The proposed legislation would once again have attempted to provide the legal framework that would bring Italy into conformity with the Schengen requirements discussed earlier. In doing so, it proposed to focus on three major areas of concern:

---

[54] See p. 48 for a discussion of the Martelli Law and the Boniver Decree.

[55] Prior to his resignation in December 1994, Prime Minister Berlusconi was also preparing to enact legislation to further restrict immigration.

[56] The commission had dismissed a set of more modest immigration proposals submitted by the government in September 1995.

(1) Seasonal agricultural workers who enter legally but typically stay on without permission;
(2) Expellable unauthorized immigrants who under current law use the 14-day grace period to destroy their documents and disappear (Italy issued almost 60,000 expulsion orders in 1994—a sixfold increase over the 1990 level of less than 10,000—but was able to carry out only about 12,000 expulsions); and
(3) Deterring the employment of foreign workers without proper permits.

In the first case, the commission proposed issuing identification cards to foreign agricultural workers authorized to work in Italy, withholding permission for their immediate families to join them for two years; it also required the workers to show that they could support those family members prior to the latter's entry. On the issue of expulsions, the proposals would authorize the government to carry out *immediate* expulsions. On the issue of the employment of unauthorized foreign workers, a system of heavy fines would be directed at those who employ such workers. In addition, heavy criminal penalties would be imposed on those who traffic in immigrants (see OECD 1995b and *Financial Times* 1995:3).

These proposals are a significant departure from the status quo, although they are quite consistent with measures adopted throughout the European space. What is most interesting about these proposals, however, is the reaction of the Party of the Democratic Left (PDS) to them *and* the apparent *denouement* of this round of Italian immigration reform. The PDS opposed the commission's proposals on a variety of fronts. It argued that the proposals rested on fundamentally weak foundations because they did not address the issue of Italy's weak border controls. More specifically, the PDS opposed the recommendations on agricultural workers on grounds that they were not taking into account a most critical fact: that Italian agriculture (and other low-wage sectors) have become dependent on foreign workers. According to the PDS, the best way to address the issue of illegal work is to focus on enforcing labor standards so as to prevent both the exploitation of unauthorized workers and the further loss of jobs to them. Implied in the PDS approach is a focus on regulating these labor markets by offering unauthorized foreign workers with stable jobs in low-wage sectors an opportunity to legalize their status, and granting authorized foreign workers in agriculture permanent residence after four years of temporary work.[57]

The PDS won some of its key points. In a decree issued by the Italian government in November 1995,[58] the PDS' viewpoints on both foreign agricultural workers and unauthorized foreign workers with steady jobs carried the day. A legalization program lasting for four months is expected to regularize the status of as many as 300,000 illegals who have been employed for at least four of the preceding twelve months (*New York Times* 1995c:7), and special provisions were created for foreign seasonal agricultural workers.[59] In addition, however, the government would be authorized to issue some permanent visas, with the number to be determined each year. The Dini government also acknowledged its dependence on the Northern League's good will by (a) providing for the immediate expulsion of foreigners convicted of crimes or considered a threat to the public order or state security by the Interior Ministry,[60] and (b) adopting 15-year imprisonment penalties for trafficking in illegal immigrants and imprisonment penalties of two to six years for those who employ illegal immigrants (see Government of Italy 1995)—the League's apparent *quid pro quo* for its support of Dini's 1996 budget. As with most compromise measures,[61] Italian institutions gave mixed reviews to the initiative. The Catholic Church objected to the "law and order" flavor of the decree, which it felt would lead to institutionalized discrimination (*New York Times* 1995c:7), while the political right was disappointed at the decree's timidness.

It is difficult to anticipate the next phase of Italy's response to immigration beyond three general observations. First, Italy's highly

---

[57] The PDS also raised serious concerns about the principle of expelling unauthorized immigrants without the benefit of appeal.

[58] The decree may be on weak constitutional grounds in that a decree implies the existence of an emergency. Since no such emergency exists, the government may be required to follow the normal route of a legislative bill (see OECD 1995b). Moreover, the decree required parliamentary approval within 60 days—a step at least delayed and possibly imperiled by the continuing political turmoil in Italy.

[59] Seasonal workers would receive 6-month work permits convertible to permanent permits if the worker receives an "open-ended" employment contract.

[60] Immigrants convicted of crimes carrying relatively short sentences would retain the right of either a legal or an administrative appeal of their expulsion order within strict timelines.

regarded corps of senior civil servants will continue to focus some attention on the issue despite the country's political implosion. Second, new legal initiatives notwithstanding, it is unrealistic to expect more than marginal gains from unilateral initiatives against unauthorized migration—given the difficulty of the task, the meager resources likely to be devoted to such an effort (the 1995 decree calls for approximately $20 million for 1996 and $40 million for 1997), the ambivalence of many of the society's key institutions about "enforcement first" strategies, and Italy's record in combatting the underground economy, where most unauthorized immigrants are employed. Third, whatever immigration initiatives are undertaken, they will continue to be influenced by the persistent north-south divide within Italy itself—which, along with immigration, has been perceived as a significant cost to the country's industrialized, wealthy north.[62]

THE TUMULTUOUS CONTEXT

Along with declines in the growth of its gross domestic product and an unemployment rate that has hovered between 11 and 12 percent throughout most of 1994 and 1995,[63] Italy's political upheaval has been accompanied by, among other things, new tensions over its immigrant communities. As in other European countries, intolerance, racism and violence against foreigners have been growing in response to cultural fears and anxieties born of encounters with a constantly diversifying immigrant presence[64]—this in a country renowned for its generosity and hospitality. A

---

[61] The decree also restricted family reunification (delay of one year and limitation to no more than two children per family as well as the requirement of ability to support).

[62] For an analysis of the historical roots of Italian politics and the future of the country in light of the theory of "path dependency," see Putnam 1993.

[63] However, according to OECD's *Economic Outlook*, "Italy's worst recession since 1975 ended in the closing months of 1993, as falling interest rates, a surprisingly good inflation performance and stronger market growth abroad began to revive business and consumer confidence. The economic expansion gathered pace in the first half of 1994, with real GDP growing at an annual rate above 3%" (OECD 1994c:73). The GDP is likely to register a similar growth in 1995 (*The European* 1995:17). Italy's withdrawal from the currency exchange-rate mechanism (ERM) of the European Community in 1992 and subsequent strategic devaluations of the lira have contributed further to the recovery as earnings from both exports and tourism have been particularly robust.

[64] As Collicelli (1995:147-150) points out, the Italian public opinion institute *Doxa* has been documenting increasingly negative Italian attitudes toward immigrants since 1987.

Rome-based group that monitors violence against foreigners in Italy estimated that in 1993 at least one hate-motivated attack on a foreigner happened every day and that the numbers rose in 1994 (*New York Times* 1995a:4). The immigration-related challenges facing Italy thus take on several dimensions, among the most significant of which are those associated with Italy's attempts to make good on its commitment to the Schengen Agreement and the Dublin Convention.[65] This means assuring the EU's persistently skeptical members that the southern part of Italy's boot has no Achilles heel to be penetrated by Africa's unemployed masses.

At the same time, Italy must remain very persuasive in making the case that it is in the EU's vital interest to continue to assign priority both to controlling unauthorized migration across the Mediterranean, Europe's Rio Grande, and to addressing the root causes of worldwide South-to-North migration. Italy can point to its own initiatives (at times taken in collaboration with other European countries) toward cooperative arrangements with countries on the Mediterranean coastline to help alleviate the growing economic and demographic gap between North Africa and the southern European flank. In an effort to lessen—albeit indirectly— emigration pressures in North Africa, Italy has in fact used both its own funds (at times in cooperation with the International Labor Organization) and EU targeted-assistance funds for employment creation and has been in the forefront of encouraging the EU to open its markets to exports from the region.

On November 27, 1995, the EU held a conference in Barcelona with twelve Southern Mediterranean countries that set the target of the year 2010 for creating an EU–Mediterranean free trade area. The event was an indication of the efforts of Italy (and others) to place the "Southern frontier" issue on an equal footing with the "Eastern frontier" on the EU's agenda. For Italy, however, it was more than that. It was a hope that the EU's far greater attention and resources would relieve Italy of some of its lonely responsibility for stemming the unwanted immigration from and through the Southern Mediterranean countries.

---

[65]Although Schengen went into effect among a core of the Agreement's signatories in the spring of 1995, Italy was not able to meet the requirements for participation. The Dublin Convention has yet to be ratified by a substantial number of EU member states, including Italy.

INSTITUTIONAL RESPONSES AND CHANGING FLOWS

IMMIGRANTS

The "Martelli Law" of February 1990, named after the then–Vice Chairman of the Italian Council of Ministers, was Italy's first comprehensive response to the migration and asylum challenge[66] (see Bisegna 1992). In addition to addressing the issue of border controls and expanding visa requirements, the act also extended and simplified an ongoing amnesty for unauthorized immigrants, emphasized the socio-cultural integration of immigrants, and extended the possibility of political asylum to all nationalities.[67] The Martelli Law was thus designed in part to synchronize Italy's policies with those of the other Schengen and EU member states, and in part to provide a framework for regulating immigration.[68]

The Martelli Law was soon followed by a more "law and order"–focused initiative, the "Boniver Decree" of March 1992, named after the then–Minister of Italians Abroad and Immigration, Margherita Boniver. The Decree detailed rules for the summary expulsion of immigrants, including asylum seekers and refugees, who lacked proper legal documentation. It also authorized police to escort aliens without visas or stay permits to the border for immediate expulsion without a court decision.

Soon after these measures were adopted, however, the turmoil surrounding Italian politics saw the elimination of the self-standing immigration portfolio and the transfer of most immigration functions to the Ministry of Labor and Social Welfare. The result was a not-unexpected loss of focus on immigration control issues. In 1993, and for much of 1994, the primary policy

---

[66]The Martelli Law began as an emergency government decree, requiring parliamentary approval within 60 days. Veugelers (1994:41) asserts that "the decree was conditioned by the foreign policy concerns of top bureaucrats, who wanted to show the EC that Italy was serious about controlling immigration."

[67]Prior to 1990, refugee status was limited to Europeans. Italy, while a signatory to the 1951 U.N. Convention relating to the Status of Refugees, had not signed the Convention's 1967 Protocol expanding the geographic coverage of the 1951 Convention beyond Europe.

[68]In addition, the law specified that refugee status could not be granted to persons who have transited a country whose government is party to the 1951 Convention (see OECD 1990:65-92). Thus, along the lines of the Dublin Convention, to which Italy became a signatory in December 1992, the law attempts to address the issue of "asylum shopping" among Europe's would-be refugees and has garnered all the associated criticisms.

emphasis was on the integration of immigrants and the continuing pursuit of the multilateral agenda—with a substantial renewal of the immigration control agenda not becoming evident again until the second half of 1994.[69]

Despite the government's considerable if uneven investment in immigration-related issues, Italy's brief experience with attempting to manage immigration is also a study in the enormous difficulties associated with establishing a central institutional locus of control over immigration matters. The Ministry for Italians Abroad and Immigration, created in April 1991, was eliminated in 1992.[70] Veugelers (1994:45) argues that the Ministry's demise should not be interpreted as "a lesser preoccupation with immigration on the part of the new government" because the previous governments' commitment was already weak. Although essentially accurate, this argument overlooks the fact that the energy for "reform" quickly dissipated with the demise of a self-standing ministry.

Today, immigration functions are distributed among the Ministries of Labor and Social Welfare, Interior, and Foreign Affairs, as well as several agencies within the Office of the Prime Minister.[71] Signaling an important reorientation of immigration activities in 1993, a new Italian commission was created within the National Council of the Economy and Labor, presided over by the Minister of Labor and Social Welfare, whose task is to focus on human rights issues regarding labor and immigration. The Commission reports directly to the presidency of the Council of Ministers. In the same spirit, the Ministry of Civil Protection has been mandated to address the issue of the growing housing shortage facing Italy's immigrants and to limit residential segregation.[72]

---

[69]In this regard, there has been significant interest in updating and strengthening the Martelli Law, particularly by those who view it as too ineffective in determining the status of refugees or in halting the entry of unauthorized immigrants (Vasta 1993:85). Although the debate is still in its early phases, proposals on a variety of issues, including the granting of residency permits and the right of foreigners to vote for local councils, were submitted to government commissions for examination. On the issue of voting for local councils, the first such elections took place in Turin in June 1995.

[70]The Ministry was responsible for Italian communities abroad, information, prevention, education and training relating to immigration, and strategic planning relating to migration flows.

[71]The diffusion of functions among many governmental agencies with multiple and diverse priorities and constituencies is common in many countries and typically tends to diminish interest in broad new initiatives. It also makes a nightmare of statistical counting and overall accountability (see Salt, Singleton, and Hogarth 1994; and Papademetriou and Hamilton 1995 for a discussion of these issues).

Most of the challenges facing these agencies are nearly a decade old and relate to the presence of a large clandestine labor force hailing primarily from North Africa. Italy's initial response was a 1987 regularization program designed to bring unauthorized immigrants into mainstream legal channels. Because of low rates of participation, the government extended the deadline for applications three times and ultimately regularized roughly 103,000 persons,[73] mainly Moroccans. A second regularization program ran from January to June 1990 and legalized the status of an additional 217,730 foreigners, leading to a dramatic increase—from 490,338 in December of 1989 to 781,138 one year later—in the number of foreigners holding a legal residence permit. Moroccans (49,860), along with Tunisians (25,474) and Senegalese (16,983), were among the largest beneficiaries, followed by Filipinos (15,240), Yugoslavs (11,320), and, at some distance, by Chinese, Egyptians, Ghanaians, Poles, Sri Lankans, Pakistanis, Somalians, and Bangladeshis (see ISTAT 1991:1-12 and OECD 1992:66). The program's relative success was attributed to increasing knowledge about it within the immigrant population and to greater efficiency on the part of the voluntary organizations and government agencies involved in providing information and assistance.

The number of residence permits issued by Italy has increased each year since the passage of the Martelli Law, although at a declining rate. The 6.9 percent increase in 1992-1993, for instance, is thus slightly lower than the 7 percent increase in 1992 and lower than all the rates during the 1980s. Italian authorities have attributed this drop to numerous factors, including a more stringent application of the Martelli Law, a weakened lira, increased unemployment, and the economic downturn.

In 1993, continuing high demand for seasonal work and the tendency of foreign workers engaged in such work to remain in the country illegally led the government to begin issuing tempo-

---

[72] Many other programs related to reception, assistance, and integration are performed by voluntary organizations.

[73] Figures reported by the Italian government regarding immigration matters should be treated cautiously. Italy's reports to the OECD frequently allude to the fact that "extreme fragmentation" in the immigration field results in a lack of consistent data (OECD 1994b:16).

rary work permits for six-month stays to seasonal workers.[74] An even more stringent system of controlling work permits was put in place in 1994 in an effort to eliminate "double registrations" and invalid permits. As a result, 88,296 work permits were canceled, mostly by eliminating multiple registrations (OECD 1994b:1).[75]

Today, most of Italy's newest immigrants come from Eastern Europe, especially from the former Yugoslavia, Romania, and Poland (see Figure 1, p.11). North African migration, primarily from the Maghreb, is declining—although the largest group of migrants is still comprised of Moroccans, Tunisians, and Senegalese. The exception to this trend are migrants from Somalia, who are treated preferentially on humanitarian grounds, partly in recognition of Italy's historical connection with that region. Filipino immigrants make up the fourth largest foreign group in Italy, numbering nearly 200,000 (*Far Eastern Economic Review* 1995:43). There are also significant numbers of Ethiopians, Egyptians, Iranians (who are among those who have resided in Italy the longest and who are considered to be the best integrated groups), and Chinese.

A final aspect of Italian immigration is a very unusual one: the return of growing numbers of ethnic Italians. While this group is composed mainly of retired individuals who have spent years working abroad—a typical "return migration"—it also includes youth of Italian extraction, especially from Latin America, where unfavorable economic conditions have swelled the flow of return migration to Italy. These young people, with few if any remaining social and cultural links to Italy, are perceived as difficult to reintegrate into Italian society (OECD 1994b:14). Similar concerns have been voiced about the return from parts of Africa of second-generation immigrants who have no ties with their parents' country of origin and who also confront an inhospitable atmosphere in Italy. These young immigrants,

---

[74]While permits are valid for only six months, foreign workers can renew them and, following two consecutive renewals, are eligible to apply for a one-year permit—provided they can prove that they have a job offer. This is a process strongly reminiscent of the guest-worker programs of the 1960s. The temporary permit entitles workers to social security benefits and maternity care and other guarantees—in theory providing some stability for the most desired workers. This is really an experiment in using the "carrot and stick" approach to regularizing seasonal workers, although it seems to ignore the tendency for temporary workers to become permanent immigrants—particularly as ethnic networks begin to dominate certain segments of the labor market. This type of response to foreign labor exemplifies the frequent tension between the needs of the economy and the stability and order that the polity prizes.

REFUGEES AND ASYLUM SEEKERS

who find themselves in a precarious condition in a country only recently coming to terms with its new identity as a receiving country, are likely to face significant integration hurdles.

As indicated in Table 3 (p.16), with the exception of 1991, when the surge of Albanians accounted for about 19,000 of that year's total of 25,472 asylum requests, Italy receives relatively few asylum claims—only 6,042 in 1992 and 1,646 in 1993 (OECD 1995a:98). Three factors account for this: (1) Italy did not accede to the 1967 Protocol to the 1951 Convention until 1990 (see also fn. 67); (2) Italian provisions for support of asylum claimants are less generous than the "benefits" offered by other EU countries; and (3) Italy generally rejects a high proportion of asylum claims.[76]

Like other European countries, Italy has shifted away from exclusive reliance on the Refugee Convention for protection ideas and resorts to other creative protection alternatives that give special consideration to extenuating circumstances and carry with them certain other rights within Italian territory. In 1992, for example, Italy offered a mini-amnesty to Somalis who did not qualify for refugee status,[77] and in December of the same year it instituted a similar program for some former Yugoslavs, in part under pressure from the Bosnian government. In addition, special residence permits have been provided to ethnically Italian Yugoslavs who have crossed into Italy. These permits allow them to work, go to school, and obtain equivalency for previous academic work and professional titles.[78]

---

[75] These multiple registrations were primarily the result of foreigners moving from one region of Italy to another and registering in various departments simultaneously.

[76] With the exception of Germany, Italy has one of the highest rejection rates for asylum applications in Europe. Of the asylum applications examined in 1993, more than 90 percent were rejected (OECD 1995a:98).

[77] This was based on an inter-ministerial decree of September 1992, which provided temporary protection to citizens from certain countries (IGC [Italy] 1994:7).

[78] Italy's rate of asylum approvals for former Yugoslavs (approximately 50 percent) is higher than that for any other group of applicants except Iraqis and Sudanese. By the end of 1994, Italy had issued approximately 83,450 humanitarian residence permits to former Yugoslavs (USCR 1995:149), and it is one of the few European countries that have not introduced visa requirements for former Yugoslavs (see Table 4, p. 20).

TOWARD INCREASING SOPHISTICATION IN POLICY AND MANAGEMENT

Significant as these exceptions are, entering Italy and obtaining refugee status is becoming more difficult, while permission to enter as a legal immigrant has been restricted primarily to those having offers of employment or joining their families.[79] Similarly, the government is making more sustained efforts to prevent unauthorized entry while at the same time intensifying surveillance and taking action against illegally resident foreigners, especially those who commit crimes.

Italy's policy responses to immigration pressures, like those of many other European countries, reveal an evolving conceptual and operational sophistication. As unwanted migration pressures from the southern Mediterranean basin become more and more palpable and the resultant immigrant population in Italy becomes larger and more visible, the need for a consistent and focused immigration policy is universally acknowledged. However, without a political system that can guarantee both constant policy attention *and* consistent implementation of laws,[80] progress can only be slow and intermittent. This seemingly inevitable disjuncture between various government initiatives and immigration developments in contemporary Italy reveals how quickly policies and institutions, and leaders and the public, can fall out of step with one another.

Like most of Europe's receiving countries, Italy has recently been focusing primarily on restrictive actions toward immigrants. This is partly in response to the politics of the Right, but it is also tied to Italy's sustained identification with the various EU processes on these issues, whose dominant feature is restrictions on immigrants of most types. The EU policy that has so far proven most politically viable has been the move toward the coordination of exclusion.

---

[79]These two categories represented 67 percent of all immigrants admitted in 1993 (OECD 1995a:98).

[80]When dealing with Italian politicians and policy-makers on this issue, one gets the impression that nearly all their energy is focused on establishing legal frameworks without as much as an acknowledgment of the administrative and management challenges that the successful implementation of legal measures present. Although this may be as it ought to be—one must first attain the legal authority to act—it is legitimate to wonder about the regime's ability to deliver measurable results on these difficult enforcement and management matters.

Part of Italy's struggle with migration stems from the inevitable policy lapses that occurred as Italy was compelled to make a remarkably quick transition from a sending to a receiving country. One of its most forward-looking and strategic responses is to focus its own and its EU partners' attention and resources on the root causes of the exodus from much of North Africa. That is a properly considered long-term strategy. It must be equally appreciated, however, that investing even substantial amounts of economic aid in sending countries (as in the cases of Albania, Poland, and some of the Maghreb countries) and calling for more multilateral involvement by the EU in these areas will not adequately meet the challenge. Extending preferential trade status to the region will go further in meeting the EU's concerns in these areas but will still prove insufficient. In fact, an externally focused policy that primarily addresses root causes simply cannot substitute for the development of responsible and sustainable internal policies and the creation of stable institutional frameworks to manage the immigration challenge at the borders and within each country.

4. THE UNITED KINGDOM: THE RELENTLESS SEARCH FOR MINIMIZING IMMIGRATION

Few countries in the EU have been as single-minded or vocal, even stubborn, as the United Kingdom about slowing the pace of European integration and resisting the expansion of the powers of Europe's central institutions. The U.K.'s assertiveness on these issues has been focused most frequently on the preservation of internal EU borders and the tightening of external ones; it reflects a long-standing and notably hard-headed posture vis-à-vis immigration and refugee/asylum matters—one that seeks to curtail all but essential immigration and to deter the filing of asylum claims.

There are several reasons behind the British policy of rigidly limiting immigration. First, such a policy comports with the image many Britons have of their country—as one that has traditionally contributed emigrants to other countries, rather than attracted or recruitted immigrants. In fact, with very few exceptions,[81] the British legal framework regarding the movement of people has accordingly focused on encouraging emigration and restricting immigration (Roche 1969). Second, even during the brief periods when the British government recruited or allowed British businesses a free hand to recruit immigrants—most notably in the late 1940s and the 1950s—it did so reluctantly. In fact, many British

---

[81] Most of these have involved Eastern European Jewish immigrants since the 1880s, sometimes significant numbers of primarily European refugees throughout the twentieth century, and the Irish. The Irish have never been subject to immigration controls and as a result have been the largest "immigrant" group in the United Kingdom. See Coleman (1994:37-40) and Salt (1995:35-36).

"IDENTITY CARDS: FREEDOM UNDER THREAT?"*

National identity cards and internal police measures to combat illegal immigration are deeply divisive issues in British political culture, primarily on privacy and civil liberties grounds, but also out of concern about the potential for such policies to lead to discrimination against the U.K.'s minorities. Nonetheless, a Green Paper was prepared in the first part of 1995 to assess whether consensus could be obtained within the government on developing a national identity card, mainly as an immigration control measure. The idea at that time was that such an identity card would at first be "voluntary" and would only become a universal requirement in phases, as people became accustomed to using it for a variety of services.

The concept received a sharp public rebuke from former Conservative Prime Minister Margaret Thatcher, speaking on behalf of the "libertarian wing" of the party. (The Conservatives' split along ideological lines mirrors the divisions on the same issue within the U.S. Republican Party, whose libertarian wing opposes such cards on privacy grounds, while its "law and order" wing sees it as a necessary evil in the broader attack against illegal immigration.) Although the identity card issue is still unresolved, the more authoritarian wing of the party seems to be committed to it; for the time being, however, it is only proceeding with a broader package of even stricter immigration and asylum controls.

Loosely fashioned after California's Proposition 187, which would deny most public benefits to illegal immigrants (and similar French proposals tabled with the EU), the package would require various individuals and organizations, such as employers, teachers, and other public servants, to inform on suspected illegal immigrants (see *The Economist* 1995g:39-40). The package also provides for withholding social security benefits from asylum applicants who make their claims *after* they enter the U.K. or those appealing a rejection (Salt 1995:84). (About two-thirds of all asylum claims filed in 1994 were made from within the U.K.) The remaining provisions focus on two initiatives. The first would create a list of "safe coun-

---

* This heading is borrowed from that of a 1995 statement by Margaret Thatcher, former British Prime Minister and head of Conservative Way Forward.

tries," (to be called a White List) that are assumed to treat their citizens properly (hence, it can be presumed that any refugee/asylum claims by such citizens would almost always be rejected with a minimum of procedure). The second initiative would institute a system to penalize employers who hire illegal immigrants.

Although the latter policy is widely in use throughout advanced industrial Europe, with little public controversy, it has created a divisive debate both within the U.K. government and among the public—despite assurances by the government that it will tread lightly in implementing the new rules. The measure has been opposed by the Education and Employment Secretary on grounds that it could increase discrimination in employment practices (and would thus adversely affect race relations and the struggle of minorities for equal employment opportunities—as employers may seek to protect themselves against possible liability by not hiring foreign-looking and -sounding individuals.) Indeed, there is already evidence of discriminatory practices, although in a slightly different form. For instance, British Airways has begun to make and keep photocopies of the passports and other papers of its minority employees.

If this debate sounds familiar to American readers, it is because it echoes U.S. debates—which retain the rancor of nearly ten years ago, when employer penalties were first adopted as an immigration control measure. It also points to a nearly inevitable "next step": As employer penalties are indeed shown to be ineffective as well as to promote discriminatory behavior, the case for national identity cards becomes stronger and more difficult to resist in the absence of a clear philosophical stance against them. The next few months will tell whether such a stance will be forthcoming—and whether it will be politically successful—in both the United States and Great Britain. *The Economist* (1995i:16) succinctly puts the case for the opposition: "[T]hese measures look suspiciously as though they are addressed less at [the U.K.'s] social problems than at the government's electoral problems. . . . [B]y promoting anti-immigrant policies, the government risks encouraging racism and undermining liberty."

opponents of immigration probably would agree with David Coleman's characterization of that period as "a fit of absence of mind" (1994:60). Third, deeply rooted beliefs in privacy and the sanctity of civil liberties have meant that British officials prefer applying exacting standards prior to entry over interior controls. This policy is aided by the geographic fact of Britain's insularity. Fourth, British officials are convinced that non-white immigration, including immigration from virtually all New Commonwealth countries,[82] is undesirable because it contributes to troubled race relations and to the potential for social conflict. The tendency to equate the obverse, minimal immigration with harmonious race relations, has deep political roots—even if it has little basis in observable reality.

Linking non-white immigration with troubled race relations has defined Tory (Conservative Party) views on immigration since 1971, when the position was first articulated as a "firm but fair" immigration policy. It was reaffirmed recently by Michael Howard, the U.K.'s Conservative Home Secretary, whose jurisdiction extends over immigration and asylum matters,[83] when he called firm immigration controls "the foundation of good race relations" (*The Guardian* 1994:9). This policy (and political) line has gone fundamentally unchallenged by the Labor Party—beyond its initial opposition to it. (A similar slogan even appeared in the Labor Party's 1987 manifesto.) In fact, even when given opportunities to reverse course on immigration in the 1970s, successive Labor governments chose not to do so (see Kaye 1994:148 and Coleman 1994:58-62). Instead, Labor chose to focus on modifying administrative rules regarding

---

[82]The *Old* Commonwealth includes Australia, Canada, and New Zealand. The *New* Commonwealth includes African countries (Botswana, Gambia, Ghana, Kenya, Kiribati, Lesotho, Malawi, Namibia, Nauru, Nigeria, Papua New Guinea, Sierra Leone, Swaziland, Tanzania, Tonga, Tuvalue, Uganda, Vanuatu, Zambia, and Zimbabwe), the Subcontinent (Bangladesh, India, Sri Lanka, and Pakistan), Malaysia, Singapore, Cyprus, the West Indies (Antigua & Barbuda, Bahamas, Barbados, Belize, Dominica, Grenada, Guyana, Jamaica, St. Kitts and Nevis, St. Vincent, the Grenadines, St. Lucia, and Trinidad & Tobago), and the island nations of Brunei, the Maldives, Mauritius, Seychelles, the Solomon Islands, Western Samoa, and Malta.

[83]Howard has pleased many right-wing Tory Members of Parliament by announcing plans to cut further both legal and illegal entry into Britain. According to *The Economist* (1995d:49), some Tory "right-wingers" want to perpetuate the myth that the U.K. is being invaded by "hordes of poor, illiterate people who are sponging off the welfare system" as a means of distinguishing themselves further from the Labor Party, which is, by virtue of some of its constituencies, more equivocal on immigration.

immigration and promoting an integration agenda that gradually became today's *de facto* multicultural policy.[84] The two major parties' habitus of acquiescing to each other's major initiatives on this issue has translated so far into both continuity in policy and an absence of electoral controversies regarding immigration. It also has meant that immigration has not been an important issue in any national electoral contest in the last two decades.

SAFEGUARDING SOVEREIGN PREROGATIVES VIS-À-VIS BRUSSELS

Running contrary to the continental majority's interpretation of the spirit of the European Union, British resistance to the Maastricht supranational "vision" is but one of several attempts to establish and maintain political and economic autonomy—not only on the traditional terrain of foreign policy but also on social and labor-market policy broadly defined. This resistance clearly builds on traditional British reluctance to surrender national sovereignty to supranational bodies of any type—a fact that is not a surprise to analysts of either British or broader European affairs. Thus, despite often enormous pressure from most EU members to move toward greater policy "concertation" on these issues, the U.K. has been unyielding.

The examples are plentiful. The British have shown no interest in the Schengen Agreement. They have been unwilling to offer any concessions to Spain on the dispute over whether Gibraltar constitutes an internal or external European frontier, and they are reluctant to accommodate any of a number of compromises on reducing border formalities for citizens of its European partners. Even more telling, the U.K. decided to "opt out" of the social clauses of the Maastricht Treaty (which include clauses relating to labor and immigration issues and subsequent initiatives in this area) and has refused to allow the European Court of Justice to gain jurisdiction over matters linked to the launching of Europol. These consistent positions constitute an explicit rejection of the concept of harmonization in migration and refugee/asylum poli-

---

[84]The legal framework for this agenda was provided by the 1965 and 1976 Race Relations acts. It is important to observe that just as Labor was reluctant to oppose immigration restrictions directly, the Conservatives have accepted the race relations framework, notwithstanding their initial opposition to it (see Coleman 1994:59-60).

cies as envisioned by many of the architects of the post-Maastricht phase of European integration.

It is important, however, to understand that Britain's carefully cultivated and aggressively maintained image of recalcitrance is also based on principle. In addition to the fundamental political objections to surrendering what it considers core sovereign functions to distant supranational authorities—a philosophical stance that is highly popular with certain constituencies at home—Britain also genuinely distrusts the instincts and objectives of Brussels on an array of issues.

In other words, Britain's steadfast position that "sensitive social and racial issues . . . should remain in the hands of national interior and justice ministers" (*The European* 1994:A1) stems from the belief that the British government, rather than the European Commission, has the better grasp of what is in the best interests of the United Kingdom. Preferring to maintain the flexibility of adjusting its own policies to respond quickly to changing immigration and asylum circumstances, Britain is hesitant to defer to the lead of Brussels. It is not, however, agnostic when it comes to the value of exchanging and vetting new ideas, especially when the orientation is toward controls. Hence, the U.K. is an active player in the EU-based intergovernmental processes that consider these issues.

SETTLEMENT ISSUES, LABOR MIGRATION, AND ASYLUM

Immigration to the U.K. declined steadily during the 1970s and the early 1980s and has remained at an annual level of 50,000-55,000 during much of the late 1980s and 1990s (OECD 1995a:126). The decline from a 1972 peak of over 90,000 to a low of 46,000 in 1987 resulted primarily from concerted statutory and administrative efforts to restrict the entitlement to settlement based on marriage and other family relationships (Salt 1994:5-6).[85] After

---

[85] The Immigration Act of 1988 repealed a provision in the Immigration Act of 1971 that had exempted the wives and children of British or other Commonwealth citizens settled in the U.K. from a probationary year of residence. In May 1990, a regulatory change required that Commonwealth citizens with a U.K.-born grandparent seeking or taking employment in the U.K. be admitted initially for four years and qualify for settlement not on arrival, as was the case previously, but only after residing in the U.K. for that period. By delaying the point at which an immigrant is counted as a permanent settler, this regulatory measure reduced the figures on permanent settlement in the early 1990s. Finally, there also have been several administrative changes to the way in which immigrants are counted. For instance, since 1986, wives and children who apply for settlement but have the right of abode are given a certificate of entitlement to that right and are no longer included in the settlement figures (U.K. Home Office 1994b:123-128).

1987, however, the numbers of those accepted for settlement rose slightly each year until 1992 and have fluctuated since.[86] Of Britain's 1,946,200 foreign-born residents in 1994, nearly 41 percent were EC nationals (see Table 1, p. 8).

Until recently, Britain's bilateral relations with many of its Commonwealth partners gave shape and predictability to much of its immigration. However, by the late 1980s, following a twenty-year effort to tighten immigration, the nature of the inflow into the U.K. began to change. According to John Salt, the United Kingdom's correspondent to the OECD, "a general picture emerge[d] of the United Kingdom as a place with diminishing numbers of new settlers, but with increasing net immigration, substantially due to rises in immigration of a more temporary nature" (OECD 1989:39). This happened despite the "closing door" policy (OECD 1990:55) toward both settlement and the substantial increases in asylum applications from non-Commonwealth sources in Africa, Asia (outside of the Indian Subcontinent), and the Middle East (Salt 1993:63).

That the British have to a large extent been able to manage, even control, immigration more effectively than most of their European partners reflects an uncommon diligence toward that goal. Despite the recent growth of temporary labor immigration and emerging concerns in some quarters about that program's "leakage into permanence," the underlying dilemma facing all industrialized countries remains a dilemma for the United Kingdom. Namely, how can the advanced industrial world fill its immediate and long-term labor needs[87]—and remain a full player in the global economy—without provoking domestic political convulsions in favor of restricting immigration?

---

[86]In 1992, there was a slight decline in acceptances (52,570), due to longer application processing times resulting from the introduction of a highly controversial and intrusive measure (which was also difficult to administer neutrally) aimed at deterring marriages whose "primary purpose" was something other than the marriage itself (Salt 1994:5-6). This was followed by an increase in 1993 (55,640), and by a decline of about 500 in 1994 (55,100). The figure for 1994 is probably artificially deflated by the fact that, as of January 1994, citizens of the European Economic Area (EEA) obtained the right to remain in the U.K. under provisions similar to those of nationals of the EU—and may thus no longer be interested in applying for settlement. The EEA is an area that includes the EU and six of the European Free Trade Association's (EFTA) seven member states (Austria, Finland, Iceland, Liechtenstein, Norway, and Sweden). (The citizens of Switzerland rejected EEA membership). Three of the EFTA states—Austria, Sweden, and Finland—have since become EU members.

[87]A significant body of opinion rejects the notion that the U.K., with an unemployed work force of about 2.3 million persons (about 8.5 percent of its population) and one of the

BRITISH IMMIGRATION POLICIES

British immigration policy is anchored in three major components: (1) a long-term work permit system; (2) a narrow refugee admissions program; and (3) a settlement system reflecting primarily post-colonial ties and, to a lesser extent, family unification linked to earlier immigration flows as well as the settlement consequences of the other two immigration components (OECD 1989:39). Labor migration has increased from a low of 15,454 in 1982 to a high in 1990 of 34,627 (OECD 1995a:127 and Salt 1995:57; see also Figure 2, p. 63).[88] Most of the increase in the number of long-term work permits occurred in the second half of the 1980s—when the numbers jumped from an average of about 6,600 per year in the 1980-86 period[89] to an average of about 12,500 per year since 1987. This increase in long-term permits primarily reflected the U.K.'s economic recovery and took place despite a persistent unemployment rate of about 9 to 10 percent (Salt & Singleton 1993:5).

The British long-term work-permit system is decidedly biased toward the highly skilled. In 1993, for instance, approximately 87 percent of the permits issued went to professional and managerial positions (Salt 1994:17).[90] Short-term work permits, whose numbers have behaved very much like those of long-term ones, continue to be concentrated in the miscellaneous services category—primarily issued to entertainers, artists, and athletes.

With the permanent exception of the Irish, who have consistently represented the largest percentage of Britain's foreign workforce,[91] the other major source countries of foreign workers have

---

highest birth rates in Europe, needs higher levels of immigration to compensate for lower cohorts of young labor force entrants (see Coleman 1994:64). That strand of opinion is expressed most forcefully by some in organized labor and its allies in and out of government who would hold firms responsible for devising and implementing training programs for indigenous (and other already permanent, if foreign-born) workers rather than permit entry of foreigners, however skilled.

[88]This includes short-term (less than one year) and long-term workers, as well as trainees.

[89]The U.K. issued far fewer foreign worker permits during the early 1980s, when unemployment was well over 10 percent.

[90]A recent Labor Force Survey reveals that, of the total stock of U.K. workers, foreign nationals are more likely to be professional, managerial, or technical workers than U.K. nationals (26.6 percent and 23 percent in 1992 and 1993, respectively) (Salt 1994:10-11).

[91]Over 28 percent of all foreign workers in the U.K. are Irish (Salt 1995:37).

Figure 2
Labor Migration to the United Kingdom, 1981–1993

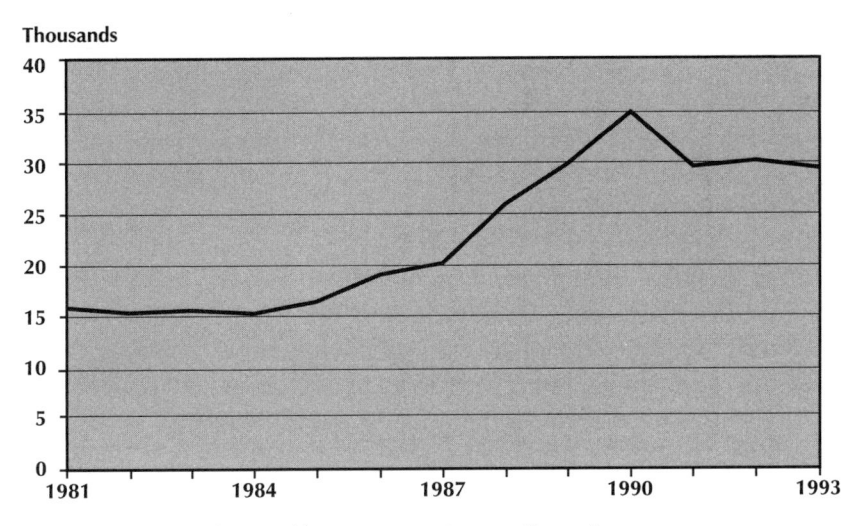

Note: Data includes short- and long-term permits, as well as trainees.
Source: John Salt, *International Migration and the United Kingdom: Report of the U.K. Correspondent to OECD—1995* (London: Migration Research Unit, University College London.)

shifted over the past decade. Moreover, consistent with the British economy's overall orientation, the non-EU, long-term foreign workforce is dominated by the United States and Japan, which together account for between 40 and 50 percent of all work permits issued from 1984 through 1994 (Salt 1994:17-18; 1995:57-59).

The British work permit system allows firms considerable flexibility to control the nature of labor immigration and to participate in the globalizing marketplace without significant impediments.[92] This is particularly important because about half of British labor immigration is accounted for by corporate transfers.[93]

---

[92] Industry's perspective on this issue is likely to be different. It is likely to see the government's efforts to regulate hiring decisions as "intrusive" attempts to micro-manage business decisions. Such contrasting views are routine, as each side would like to pursue *its* own policy goals relatively unimpeded.

[93] Changes to the work permit system introduced in October 1991 were designed to facilitate further intra-company transfers. In 1994, 51 percent of all work permits were issued to corporate transfers (Salt and Singleton 1993:8-9; Salt 1995:59).

Approximately one-third of newly entering foreign workers are under 25 years of age, and, during 1993-94, 84 percent were under the age of 35. European Union workers, most of whom are in service employment (primarily hotel and catering work), tend to be particularly concentrated in the younger age groups; indeed, in 1994, 92 percent of those who entered the U.K. from other EU member states were under the age of 35; 57 percent were 18 to 24 years old (Salt 1995:40, 52).[94]

Despite a work permit system that strongly emphasizes the highly skilled, some critics assert that the government's negative attitude toward immigration has sold the country short. It has "failed to reap the economic benefits from selective skilled migration, foregone the investment and jobs which entrepreneurs could provide, and prevented companies from benefiting fully from intra-company transfers" (*Financial Times* 1994a:16). The protectionist tendencies of British immigration law, these critics charge, run counter to what many economists and some policy analysts believe would enhance the country's well-being.

DETERRING ASYLUM CLAIMS

Although Britain has not been immune to the EU's asylum "crisis," its increase in asylum applications has been mitigated by geography, close administrative attention to these applications, and legislation. During most of the 1980s, there were fewer than 5,000 asylum applications per year. In 1989, however, the numbers rose to 11,640, and they peaked at about 45,000 (excluding dependents) in 1991. In 1992 and 1993, applications dropped dramatically (to 24,605 and 22,370, respectively), and they have been on an upward swing since then—registering 32,835 in 1994 and projected at more than 40,000 in 1995 (see Table 3, p. 16, and Salt 1995:72-76). The largest applicant groups in 1993 were from

---

[94]Employment in tourism and recreation, as well as in the health and education sectors, are the very areas in which forecasters expect major job gains (Salt, *et al.* 1994:170). Yet, long-term work permits issued for catering and personal services fell sharply in 1993. The interpretation of this and other labor migration trends is not easy. The changes in 1993 may be a consequence of the introduction of modifications to the work permit system in October 1991 and of the likely delays before their full implementation. The trend may also reflect changes in the recruitment policies of companies and new ways of acquiring high-level skills and expertise (Salt 1994:17).

Sri Lanka, the former Yugoslavia, Ghana, Nigeria, Turkey, Somalia, and India (U.K. Home Office 1994a:4). Of the 1994 applicants, Africans made the greatest share of the claims (50 percent), followed by Asians (almost 30 percent)—a trend that continued in 1995. In both years, Nigerians were the largest applicant nationality, accounting for 4,340 in 1994 and projected to account for 6,210 in 1995.[95] The next two largest nationalities were Sri Lankans and Turks in 1994, and Indians and Somalis in 1995 (see Salt 1995:73, 78).

The case of asylum seekers from the former Yugoslavia is indicative of the effort the British government devotes to controlling access to the United Kingdom. Until late 1992, the U.K. was in the forefront of a concerted Western European effort to discourage those fleeing the various conflicts in the former Yugoslavia from leaving protected areas there.[96] That effort was implemented rigidly by the humanitarian agencies operating in the former Yugoslavia, including the UNHCR, on the theory that those displaced by these conflicts would be more easily reintegrated if they were not sent to third countries. The policy's effect, however, was that most Western European governments did not feel the same pressure to resolve the conflicts as they would have had large numbers of refugees fled to their countries. For a variety of rea-

---

[95]Britain's response to the increase in asylum applications by Nigerians has been swift and, in the eyes of the government's critics, nothing less than unconscionable. The U.K. has added Nigeria (along with China and Ghana) to its list of countries whose nationals not only require a visa to travel to the U.K., but also require a transit visa to enter the U.K. en route to another country; the list already included the nationals of Afghanistan, Iran, Iraq, Libya, Somalia, Sri Lanka, Turkey, Uganda, and Zaire (Salt 1995:85). Furthermore, the U.K. it has rejected all but one of the asylum claims of Nigerians it adjudicated during the first eleven months of 1995, and it is proposing to include Nigeria in its White List of safe countries of origin.

[96]The number of former Yugoslavs applying for asylum stood at 15 per year for 1989 and 1990, increased to 320 in 1991, and to 5,635 in 1992. Requests declined to 1,830 in 1993. They declined further to 1,385 in 1994 and rose somewhat to 1,510 in 1995 (Salt 1995:82). Due mainly to domestic and international pressure, the British government agreed in November 1992 to accept another 4,000 persons from the former Yugoslavia, including 1,000 ex-detainees from Bosnia, on an "exceptional leave" basis for a period of six months. While agreeing to increase its admission of Bosnians, the U.K. simultaneously imposed a visa requirement for nationals of the former Yugoslavia (except Croatians and Slovenians). However, the U.K. does not have a consulate in Sarajevo and operates its consulates in Zagreb and Belgrade with a very limited staff (*Manchester Guardian Weekly* 1992:12). Limiting visa-issuing capabilities in a country is not an unusual means of regulating the access of that country's nationals to another.

sons, Austria, Germany, Sweden, and Switzerland[97] were thus left to shoulder most of the burden of refugees from that area. Austria and Germany have received more than half a million officially, with many more thought to be in these countries unregistered. Switzerland has received close to 70,000, while Sweden has received almost 115,000—although the number of new claimants to Sweden has dropped dramatically since it imposed visa requirements for Bosnians in 1994 (see Table 3, p. 16).

Since for most asylum seekers the U.K. is a distant and insular point of entry, the majority must first pass through another country. The U.K. takes full advantage of that by implementing the "safe-third-country" concept,[98] first developed in the as yet unratified Dublin Convention. In addition, since 1987, the U.K. has fined carriers over £80 million for carrying passengers with insufficient travel documents.[99]

Reliance on a strict visa regime has been another frequently used and largely successful method of British control. For instance, in response to growing numbers of requests for asylum by a specific nationality, the U.K. routinely imposes visa requirements on citizens of these countries; this typically results in a significant drop in the number of asylum applications.[100] In other cases, the scrutiny of the visa issuance process and the cost of the visa have been significant deterrents to applying for asylum in the United Kingdom.

Moreover, the U.K. has adopted new statutory measures to tighten access to asylum and further restrict immigration. After a

---

[97]Sweden's reluctance to impose a visa requirement earlier reflects the political reality that a very sizable community of ethnic Yugoslavs already resides in Sweden. That community and its political allies had effectively advocated in favor of a tolerant policy toward refugees from the warring regions. Similar reasons, in addition to geography (and, at least for Germany, its historic relationship to Croatia), account for the large presence of former Yugoslavs in the other three countries.

[98]This allows British officials to turn back asylum applicants who have transited through another country—the "third" country in this formulation—that meets such criteria as having signed certain refugee protection instruments and having an asylum claim adjudication apparatus. This concept should not be confused with the "safe-country-of-origin" one for which the U.K. is developing the White List of countries discussed earlier.

[99]In 1991, Britain doubled carrier fines to £2,000 per undocumented passenger.

[100]For instance, the U.K. imposed visa requirements for Turks on June 23, 1989. This action led to a drop in Turkish asylum applications from 2,415 in 1989 to 1,590 in 1990. In the Ugandan case, where the visa requirement was imposed on April 2, 1991, applications dropped from 2,125 in 1990, to 1,450 in 1991, and to 295 in 1992. In another instance—one involving Haitians—the action had more of a preemptive character.

protracted and divisive debate, the U.K. enacted the Asylum and Immigration Appeals Act of July 1993. The Act provides for a fast-track (28-day) procedure for "unfounded" claims—another of the Dublin Convention's key features. It also introduces the right of appeal for applicants who are refused asylum but imposes time limits for all stages of the application and appeals processes (U.K. Home Office 1995b:17). Furthermore, the U.K. has instituted a policy of detaining at ports of entry those applicants filing asylum claims deemed by immigration officers to be "manifestly unfounded"[101]—another attempt to deter would-be asylum seekers from demanding refuge in the U.K.

Finally, the U.K. also offers an "exceptional leave to remain" (ELR) status. This option is available to those asylum seekers who do not conform to the 1951 Convention's definition of a refugee yet have compelling reasons for not being returned to their country (USCR 1994:154). This status, which must be renewed annually (and is in several respects similar to the United States' Temporary Protected Status and Parole grants), provides for family unification after four years and settlement after seven.[102] While grants of ELR increased from 36 percent of total decisions in 1991 to 48 percent in 1993, they decreased to 17 percent in 1994 (USCR 1995:170; Salt 1995:79).

It is still too early to assess whether the more stringent measures adopted in the past few years will in the long run have the desired effect of controlling the number of applications and streamlining the decision-making process. Lag time in implementing the new asylum legislation had made the backlog of pending asylum cases climb to more than 50,000 by mid-1995. These facts have led some to question whether the streamlining process has been as effective as intended. Others worry about the "time bomb" of pending asylum appeals from earlier times. Still others point to the continuing lack of coordination between control and adjudication functions (which are divided between the Home and Justice Ministries) and predict an administrative breakdown of that part of the process.

---

[101] Asylum refusals fall into three categories: (a) the applicant fails to meet the criteria of the 1951 Convention definition of a refugee; (b) the applicant has crossed a "safe" third country; and (c) the applicant is unable to provide sufficient evidence to support a claim within a specified period of time. In 1994, 3.9 percent of the asylum claims processed were granted "Convention" status (U.K. Home Office 1995a:Table 4.1).

[102] In contrast, full refugee status allows recipients immediate family reunification rights and the right to apply for settlement after four years.

The U.K.'s strategy to date of relying primarily on pre-entry rather than post-entry controls[103] both underscores and sustains the U.K.'s resolute opposition to abolishing internal EU frontiers and its interest in the strongest possible EU external border controls. Given this stance, it is not surprising that, when the U.K. held the EU presidency (during the second half of 1992), two of its priorities on these issues were restricting asylum claims and seeking agreement on eliminating labor migration. Indeed, it was during that year's London Council that a variety of restrictive measures received their initial EU-wide review. These included resolutions regarding "host third countries" and "manifestly unfounded applications for asylum," conclusions regarding "countries in which there is generally no serious risk of persecution," and recommendations regarding "practices followed by Member States on expulsion" and "transit for the purposes of expulsion" (see Papademetriou 1996 for a discussion of the London Council and these terms of art).

TIGHTENING NATURALIZATION AND CITIZENSHIP REQUIREMENTS

The U.K. has also implemented a series of changes restricting naturalization and citizenship. The British Nationality Act of 1981 (which became effective on January 1, 1983), provides that residency rights will "in due course . . . depend exclusively on the possession of British citizenship" (U.K. Home Office 1992:88).[104] While the law extends transitional citizenship benefits to some applicants,[105] it also limits the entitlement to citizenship of others.[106]

---

[103]As discussed earlier, the government is seeking legal authority to focus equally on post-entry controls.

[104]The British Nationality Act of 1981 defines British citizenship, British Overseas citizenship, British Dependent Territories citizenship, and two related categories—British protected persons and British subjects.

[105]The British Nationality Act of 1981 significantly reduced the number of persons eligible for British citizenship. Yet many persons did not apply for citizenship until 1987, when the transitional provisions of the Act were about to end—"a consequence of one of those rushes to 'beat the deadline' that have characterized British immigration policy over several decades" (Salt 1990:72).

[106]The 1981 Act requires that the wife of a husband seeking settlement be a British citizen and provides that children born in the U.K. after January 1, 1983, cannot acquire British citizenship unless at least one parent is either settled in the U.K. or a British citizen at the time of the child's birth. Citizenship is granted to the child once either parent becomes a citizen and upon application by the child (U.K. Home Office 1992:88-89).

In 1993, British citizenship was granted to 45,800 persons—a 9 percent increase over the previous year, although still below the level of each year since 1987. The number for 1994 stood at 44,000—a decrease of 4 percent. Most of the drop since 1990 has been among New Commonwealth citizens, whose access to citizenship has been severely curtailed under the British Nationality Act. As a result, only about two-fifths of the naturalizations in both 1993 and 1994 were for citizens of those countries, compared to about seven-tenths in the late 1980s (OECD 1995a:228).[107]

A large part of the effort to restrict access to British citizenship has focused on making citizenship increasingly dependent on "discretionary" rather than "entitlement" grounds. For instance, of the 44,033 grants of citizenship in 1994, only 6,236 were granted on the basis of entitlement (largely limited to the wives of British citizens married prior to 1983 and to individuals meeting certain residency qualifications). Instead, most citizenship grants were based on marriage to a British citizen (14,933) or on residency qualifications or relevant employment grounds (15,591) (Salt 1995:32)—i.e., grounds over which British authorities have, theoretically at least, considerable administrative control. Grants to settlers from *non*-Commonwealth countries have increased as a proportion of the total.

BRITAIN'S TROUBLED RACE AND ETHNIC RELATIONS

Unlike some other European countries, the U.K. has long accepted that it is involved in a continuing process of *de facto* immigration that can, if mismanaged, push the issue to the forefront of the political agenda. One of the topics that constantly keeps immigration near the political forefront is racial tensions between ethnic[108] and majority communities. "Integration" in the U.K. has thus become synonymous with race relations (Fitzgerald 1993:3).

---

[107]In addition to the grants of citizenship in the U.K., large numbers of persons have been granted British citizenship in Hong Kong under the British Nationality Hong Kong Act of 1990: 48,700 in 1992, 41,800 in 1993, and 51,900 in 1994 (OECD 1995a:127 and Salt 1995:31).

[108]"Ethnic" is not coterminous with "immigrant" in this usage. The 1991 census (which, for the first time, included a question regarding ethnicity), found that 46.8 percent of the U.K.'s "ethnic" population was born in the United Kingdom (Salt 1993:15).

While the U.K. has actively engaged the integration issue since the 1960s, its responses to substantial waves of anti-immigrant and anti-foreign activism and violence have been intermittent, generally *ad hoc*, and of questionable effectiveness. After one of the earliest instances of such violence, the murder of a Jamaican immigrant in 1958, the government reacted by instituting stricter immigration controls. By the mid-1960s, however, the government had acknowledged its race relations problem and passed the Race Relations Acts of 1965 and 1968. A third Race Relations Act was passed in 1976, establishing the Commission for Racial Equality.[109] That Commission was made "responsible both for the application of anti-discrimination legislation and for a range of social, educational, and informational activities aimed at eliminating racial discrimination and promoting better community relations" (Council of Europe 1991:12).[110]

These initiatives, however, have not apparently resulted in substantial improvements in race relations. Surveys conducted during the 1980s revealed that 9 out of 10 persons acknowledged that racial prejudice is prevalent in Britain, and about one-third admitted to having such prejudices (Oakley 1992:16). In 1981, following many years of pressure from advocacy groups, the government conducted the first official study of the incidence of racial attacks in Britain.[111]

The national study, which surveyed inter-racial incidents recorded by the police, revealed that blacks were the main victims, while West Indians and Asians (referring to people from the Indian Subcontinent) were, respectively, 36 and 50 times more likely to be attacked than whites. Another report issued that same year by the Commission for Racial Equality documented the continuing problem of serious discrimination in public housing—with an emphasis on the more subtle forms of harassment that are not

---

[109]As mentioned earlier, the approach to race relations embodied in these acts reflects the Labor Party's main contribution to the "immigration issue."

[110]The 1976 Act also provided for "positive action" programs for tackling indirect forms of institutional discrimination and called upon local government to play a role in combating racial discrimination and inequality in areas such as public housing, education, and employment (Oakley 1992:16).

[111]While incidents of harassment have existed for a long time in Britain, punctuated by such particularly serious events as the murder of the Jamaican immigrant in 1958 and the "Paki-bashing" incidents of the mid-60s, this study offered the first "official" recognition of the situation.

dealt with under criminal law. The report highlighted the damaging consequences of such discrimination for the successful integration of Britain's ethnic communities.[112]

In 1989, a report by an inter-departmental working party of central government officials recommended the adoption of a "multi-agency approach" to combat racial violence and harassment. In some localities, particularly London, local multi-agency panels have been active in such efforts for several years. However, eliminating racism arising from social and economic circumstances is beyond the means of local agencies. A 1987 Commission for Racial Equality report, *Living with Terror*, revealed that few housing authorities had adequately implemented policies against housing discrimination. The Commission used the race-based murder of an Asian youth in a Manchester high school as an example of how "counter-productive" and dangerous improperly executed anti-racist policies can be (Oakley 1992:20-21).

Britain continues to experience serious domestic tensions regarding its ethnic communities—despite its relatively long history of engaging the issue and efforts to ensure that everyone "participates freely and fully in the economic, social and public life of the nation while having the freedom to maintain their own religious and cultural identity" (Council of Europe 1991:12). In 1990, for instance, a government proposal to consider offering immigration benefits to 50,000 Hong Kong Chinese families closely connected with Britain's administration of the colony prior to 1997 (when Hong Kong will revert to China) met with a public outcry. Some conservatives argued that Britain has "had a massive amount of immigration for 30 years and people have had enough" (*New York Times* 1990:1).[113] In 1992, nearly 8,000 racial attacks were reported in the United Kingdom—well over three times the number reported in Germany, where the phenomenon has received far greater attention.

As elsewhere in Europe, the political resonance of anti-immigrant sentiment in the U.K. has been exploited electorally, if in a

---

[112] A report by the Strasbourg-based Council of Europe pointed out the implications of such violence "for a successful integration policy" and noted that racial violence and harassment have been used as "a means of maintaining racial segregation and white domination especially in the more desirable residential zones" (Oakley 1992:17).

[113] According to the *New York Times* (1990:1), there are over 3 million British passport holders in Hong Kong.

controlled way. In October 1993, nearly a quarter of a century after then-Member of Parliament Enoch Powell turned immigration and race into a political career, Britons elected another anti-immigrant demagogue, this time to a local London Council seat. Derek Beackon, a candidate of the far-Right British National Party (BNP), which advocates "rights for whites" and the forced repatriation of non-whites, won 30 percent of the vote in the East London borough of Tower Hamlets. Post-election comments indicated that "most of those who voted for him did so to protest the shortage of adequate public housing in the area and to register their unhappiness with expenditures made by the financially hard-pressed Labor-dominated Council in order to integrate the district's impoverished Bangladeshi immigrant community" (Gelb 1993:5-6). This, coupled with "off the cuff" comments made by Bernie Grant, a British MP and the most prominent black spokesman—comments implying that British blacks should be given the option of returning to their countries of origin with financial assistance from the government (Gelb 1993:5-6)—and the subsequent outcry from the black community, highlights Britain's troubled race relations.

PERSISTENT PATTERNS AND POLICIES

The British case illustrates the resilience of immigration policies as well as the uphill battle that governments face in balancing the competing demands of immigration and the challenges of integration and tolerance. A focus on policies alone does not, however, reveal the very real impact that immigration policies have on the lives of immigrants. Similarly, a focus on statistics tells little about the political context in which policies are designed and executed. The British government's preoccupation with numbers has also led to some unfortunate excursions into "smoke and mirrors" territory. For instance, little is gained *in the long term* by manipulating the numbers to portray backlog processing as new rejections, or by implementing administrative changes regarding who will be counted as an immigrant and when. Yet British policy-makers apparently think that they benefit if such measures allow them to appear to be responding to popular sentiment to reduce immigration further, or if administrative and policy ambiguities discourage, or even deter, some potential applicants.

In fact, the actual numerical effect of the ever-tightening immigration restrictions has been relatively modest. This may reflect a reluctance by the government to engage in a four-sided political battle with ethnic communities, liberals, industry, and some of its own conservatives. Attempts to avoid this confrontation are evident in the contrast between the U.K.'s stringent initial-entry screens and its more easily "breached" standards for eventual immigration or for converting long-term temporary workers into permanent immigrants. This latter type of "back door" immigration allows the U.K. to be highly selective in its employment-based immigration while continuing its public stance in favor of reducing all immigration.

Despite the U.K.'s attempts to—within political and economic limits—close down all but "essential" immigration channels, race and community-relations tensions have become permanent features of domestic British politics. In the next few years, many governments, including Britain's, can be expected to regulate immigration ever more stringently in response to popular reservations about it. At the same time, strong legislation protecting the rights of immigrants within a receiving country's borders is likely to become as necessary as efforts to protect human rights abroad.

5. CONCLUSION: TRENDS AND LESSONS

As major players in the ongoing European immigration drama, France, Italy, and the U.K. exemplify the improvisational character of governmental responses to the new political theater of immigration and asylum. Their responses signal the changing fortunes of immigration. Today's preoccupation with entry and interior controls and the removal of unauthorized immigrants contrasts starkly with the preceding two decades of generous "regularization" programs and corresponding policies emphasizing the rights of *all* immigrants, regardless of legal status.

Two other trends are also striking. First, mainstream political parties have been quite adept at keeping immigration and refugee/asylum issues from becoming the focus of national election campaigns. The parties have done so primarily by adopting central elements of the fringe's agenda—thus removing it from the policy debate and thereby denying it political space—and by avoiding public confrontations among themselves on key aspects of immigration and refugee policy. Considering the issue's volatility, this dual tactic of appeasing the extreme Right while refraining from "leading" on this issue has been remarkably successful. Yet the arrangement is unstable. Its limitations became evident during the most recent French elections, when the Le Pen agenda nearly dominated the first round of voting. This suggests that mainstream political parties may have to rediscover the importance—if not the necessity—of leading on critical public policy issues, however divisive some of those issues may be. Second, there is a growing disjuncture between (1) initiatives motivated by "law and order" concerns and increasingly restrictionist impulses, including initiatives that withhold certain rights and privileges from immigrants and (2) practical efforts to improve the integration of immigrants at the local level. Too often, the contradictions between the two go unnoticed. *De facto* integration is continuing apace with a myriad of mundane individual everyday acts—from intermarriages to hiring decisions by private firms that wish to make efficient use of diverse workforces. The long-term social and economic lives of communities rest on these everyday matters. Communities continue to adapt to the reality of diversity by searching for the most effective ways of incorporating immigrants. This is typically done outside the glare of the political floodlights, which tend to fall on problem areas rather than modest success stories.

Clearly, these trends require continuing exploration. The increasingly complex relationship between the exclusionary policies and anti-immigration rhetoric of politicians and the reality of on-the-ground mutual accommodations between hosts and newcomers—not all of which are smooth—suggests the next area for both analytical and policy focus. Recognizing the common challenges that face all diverse societies might be a good starting point. Integration is the fulcrum on which societies ultimately balance; *successful* societies in the next century must resolve the integration puzzle and address the admissions/integration nexus more conscientiously than they have to date.

Thus, the lessons to be drawn from the experiences of these three countries are far broader than may be suggested by this essay's concern with the convergence of European policies toward tighter controls and greater restriction. Four main lessons emerge.

1. It is difficult for governments to rewrite history. The migration experiences of both France and the U.K., and to some degree Italy, are to a large extent shaped by the links established during a period of European imperial expansion and by these countries' current roles as major global economic actors. Historically, migration flows have run from core to peripheral countries—initially to implant a colonial presence to exploit resources, and to find cheap labor and open markets. In recent decades, however, the tide has reversed as immigrants from the South and East have sought to settle in the urban centers of Western Europe, many following the long-established routes of earlier relationships.

These new flows, like their predecessors, are and will continue to be woven into the network of global economic relations. France, the U.K., and even Italy cannot rewrite their imperial pasts or deny their current economic interests, but they find it very hard to live with some of the immigration consequences of these forces. Italy suffers the additional handicap of having to cope with a veritable political revolution while attempting to write the early chapters of its own history as a *receiving* country. Although it stands to gain considerable insights from the experience of its European partners on these issues, Italy seems quite unlikely to avoid their mistakes and failures.

2. Ethnic diversity and integration are part and parcel of immigration policy. Of the three countries whose policies are reviewed here, the U.K. appears to be the most successful in restricting immigration. Its experience, however, may illustrate how difficult it is to contain ethnic and racial animosities and promote integration while political discourse portrays new Commonwealth immigration as a mistake and the government invests extraordinary effort and resources in restricting it as tightly as possible.

More broadly, divisive debates over citizenship and asylum issues are beginning to undermine the willingness of receiving states to grant immigrant and refugee populations from new source countries full and permanent access to the political, social, and economic resources implied by permanent membership in modern democratic societies. France faces the additional challenge of domestic turmoil over the proper role of Islam—ushered in and embedded within French society by immigrant communities directly linked to the country's colonial past—in a strongly secular state. Only when receiving countries make sense of their increasing social, ethnic, and religious diversity—and develop their own practical models of pluralism—will the social and cultural problems so often associated with immigration and its effects on national identity stand a chance of being diminished.

3. The politics of immigration is also in part the politics of the European Union and its reception in individual countries. Italy, in its desire to allay the concerns of the U.K. and some of its other EU partners about the permeability of its borders, has been eager to promote and work within the ambit of an EU-wide approach to immigration. At some level, the more the EU embraces a strategy of comprehensive controls and other initiatives designed to reduce immigration (including the promotion of the "South's" economic development), the less pressure there is on Italy to take—and effectively implement—extraordinary measures to control its own porous borders. The U.K., for obverse reasons, is reluctant to relinquish its own brand of controls to the EU, fearing that EU recipes will be simultaneously weak and insensitive.

In France, too, the EU plays into the immigration debate, although the terms of France's engagement are distinct. Many in France feel that their national prerogatives in this area will be curtailed if they are transferred to Brussels. The troubled Schengen experiment reinforces that view. Simultaneously, some politicians of the Left point to the EU—not to immigrants—as the most powerful challenge to French autonomy and stability.

4. A rational immigration policy and political stability are linked. In the absence of an effectively functioning political system, it is very difficult to achieve coherence, continuity, and policy success on immigration. Dysfunctional governments magnify the tensions that typically exist within governmental bureaucracies about the proper tone, emphasis, and priority that immigration issues demand. Similarly, it is extraordinarily arduous to make and implement thoughtful and progressive policy decisions when a society is buffeted by fundamental and disorderly change. The perception of political threats (as in the case of France vis-à-vis Algeria) further diminishes the probability for well-considered policies. Finally, attempting to use immigration policy to achieve other domestic or foreign policy goals (such as European integration, or assisting the development of Third World countries) pins the success of one difficult set of initiatives to that of another and multiplies the chances for failure. Immigration policy then suffers accordingly.

These observations are not a condemnation of the immigration policy efforts of France, Italy, and the United Kingdom. They are simply a reminder that good policy is the product of sound analysis, clear goals, clear rules, and appropriate legislative and regulatory tools. These are the tests that all three countries have yet to pass.

REFERENCES

Note: Throughout this paper, English translations from French language references are ours.

Barsotti, Odo, and Laura Lecchini. 1994. "Social and Economic Aspects of Foreign Immigration to Italy," in *European Migration in the Late Twentieth Century,* Heinz Fassmann and Rainer Münz (eds.). Aldershot, Hants, England: Edward Elgar Publishing, Ltd., for International Institute for Applied Systems Analysis (IIASA), Laxenburg, Austria.

Bisegna, Clara. 1992. *"La Politica dell'Immigrazione,"* in *La Italia nella Politica Internazionale.* Milan: Istituto Affari Internazionali.

Boyzon-Fradet, Danielle. 1992. "The French Education System: Springboard or Obstacle to Integration?" in *Immigrants in Two Democracies: French and American Experience,* D. Horowitz and G. Noiriel (eds.). New York: New York University Press.

Brubaker, William Rogers. 1989. *Immigration and the Politics of Citizenship in Europe and North America.* New York: University Press of America.

Césari, Jocelyne. 1994. *Être Musulman en France: Associations, militants, et mosquées. Collection hommes et sociétés.* Paris: Karthada.

Coleman, David A. 1993. "The World on the Move? International Migration in 1992," in *European Population Conference Proceedings, Vol. 1.* Geneva: United Nations Economic Commission for Europe, Council of Europe, and United Nations Population Fund.

———. 1994. "The United Kingdom and International Migration: A Changing Balance," in *European Migration in the Late Twentieth Century,* Heinz Fassmann and Rainer Münz (eds.). Aldershot, Hants, England: Edward Elgar Publishing, Ltd., for International Institute for Applied Systems Analysis (IIASA), Laxenburg, Austria.

Collicelli, Carla. 1995. "Immigration and Cultural Anxiety in Italy," in *Affari Sociali Internazionali,* No. 2.

Council of Europe. 1991. *Community and Ethnic Relations in Europe.* Final report of the Community Relations Project of the Council of Europe. Strasbourg: Council of Europe.

Decouflé, André-Clément, and Martine Tétaud. 1993. *La Politique de la Nationalité en 1992.* Paris: Ministère des Affaires Sociales, de la Santé et de la Ville, Direction de la Population et des Migrations.

The Economist. 1990. "Shame on Britain." August 4:42.

———. 1991. "Is Europe's boat full?" August 17:41.

———. 1993. "Until the Fat Lady Sings. A Survey of Italy." June 26:1-22.

———. 1995a. "France and European Union: Southward Swing." January 14:45-46.

———. 1995b. "France: The Far Right Factor." March 4:53.

———. 1995c. "French Unemployment: The 12% Shame." April 1:42.

———. 1995d. "Rivers of Bluster." April 1:49.

———. 1995e. "Locals Love Le Pen." June 17:53.

———. 1995f. "Clean Dirt." June 24:48-52.

———. 1995g. "Britain: Excessive Use of Force." July 15:39-40.

———. 1995h. "France Prepares for EMU." December 9:11-12.

———. 1995i. "Political Asylum in Britain." December 9:16.

———. 1995j. "The Challenge to EMU: Europe learns the alphabet." December 9:19-21.

———. 1995k, "The strength in Juppé's inability to yield." December 9:49-50.

The European. 1994. Roy Watson and Victor Smart, "EU Split over Charter for Migrant Rights." February 4-10:A1.

———. 1995. "Country Data." December 7-13:17.

European Information Network (EIN). 1995. *Migration News Sheet* (March). Brussels: EIN.

Far Eastern Economic Review. 1995. "A New Kind of Hero." March 30:43.

Financial Times. 1992. Edward Mortimer. "Pass the Human Parcel." December 9:17.

———. 1994a. Edward Mortimer. "Free to be held Captive." May 4:16.

———. 1994b. Francis Ghiles. "Unease inside Moslem Paris." September 1:3.

———. 1995. Robert Graham. "Italian Parties start to turn the spotlight on illegal immigrants." October 14:3.

Fitzgerald, Marian. 1993. "Integration: The U.K. Experience." Paper presented at the Conference of the Organisation for Economic Cooperation and Development (OECD), held in Madrid, Spain, March 29.

Foreign Broadcast Information Service. 1994a. "INSEE Issues Comprehensive Immigration Study," *Le Monde*, June 10:16, cited in *West Europe*. Washington, DC: FBIS, July 12 (FBIS-WEU-94-133):29-30.

———. 1994b. "Immigration Agreement Denounced," Radio France International, November 4, cited in *West Europe*. Washington, DC: FBIS, November 7 (FBIS-WEU-94-215):22.

———. 1995. "EU Leaders Reach Agreement at Cannes Summit," Agence France Presse, June 27, cited in *West Europe*, Washington, DC: FBIS, June 27 (FBIS-WEU-94-123):1.

Garson, Jean-Pierre. 1992. "Immigration and Interdependence: The Migration System between France and Africa," in *International Migration Systems: A Global Approach.* Mary Kritz, et al. (eds.). New York: Oxford University Press.

Gelb, Norman. 1993. "Repatriation vs. Integration: The Ugly Face of British Racism." *The New Leader* (November 15-29):5-6.

Government of Italy. 1995. *Decree Law on Immigration.*

The Guardian. 1994. Michael White. "Euro-Campaign Heats up as Tories Play 'Race Card'." May 27:9.

———. 1995. Alan Travis and Stephen Bates. "ID Card Idea to be fought by Tory Right." May 12:5.

Hamilton, Kimberly. 1994. Personal Interview conducted with Jean-Claude Barreau, former director of the Office of International Migration. July 1, 1994.

Hoffmann, Stanley. 1993. "Thoughts on the French Nation Today." *Daedalus,* 122 (Summer):63-79.

Horowitz, Donald. 1992. "Immigration and Group Relations in France and America," in *Immigrants in Two Democracies: French and American Experience,* D. Horowitz and G. Noiriel (eds.). New York: New York University Press.

Institut National de la Statistique et des Études Économiques (INSEE). 1992. *Recensement de la Population de 1990, Nationalités, Resultats du sondage au quart.* Paris: INSEE.

———. 1994. *Les Étrangers en France.* Paris: INSEE.

Istituto Nazionale di Statistica (ISTAT). 1991. "*La presenza straniera in Italia,*" *Notiziario, Serie* 4, *Foglio* 41, *Anno* XII, No. 5 (March).

Kaye, Ronald. 1994. "Defining the Agenda: British Refugee Policy and the Role of Parties," in *Journal of Refugee Studies* 7, No. 2/3:144-159

Lebon, André. 1992. *Aspects de l'immigration et de la présence étrangère en France, 1991-1992.* Paris: *Ministère des Affaires Sociales et de l'Integration.*

———. 1993. *Aspects de l'Immigration et de la Présence Étrangère en France, 1992-1993.* Paris: *Ministère des Affaires Sociales et de l'Integration.*

———. 1994. *Situation de l'Immigration et de la Présence Étrangère en France, 1993-1994.* Paris: *Ministère des Affaires Sociales et de l'Integration.*

Manchester Guardian Weekly. 1992. "Have Visa but Can't Travel." November 15:12.

Marie, Claude-Valentin. 1994. "From the Campaign Against Illegal Migration to the Campaign Against Illegal Work" (translated from the French by Mark Miller), in *Annals,* AAPSS, No. 534 (July):118-132.

Martin, David. 1989. "Effects of International Law on Migration Policy and Practice: The Uses of Hypocrisy," in *International Migration Review* 23, No. 3:547-578.

Moreau, Gerard. 1994. Presentation delivered at an International Migration Policy Program Policy Briefing at the Carnegie Endowment for International Peace, Washington, DC, April 26.

New York Times. 1990. Craig Whitney. "Big British Fight Shapes up on Hong Kong Emigré Plan." January 10:1.

———. 1991. Associated Press. "Paris Ousts Civil Servant for Book on Islam." November 13:3.

———. 1994. Youssef M. Ibrahim. "France Bans Muslim Scarf in Schools." September 11:4.

———. 1995a. John Tagliabue. "Sunny Italy Turns a Scowling Face to Immigrants." January 5:4.

———. 1995b. Craig Whitney. "Rightists Play Immigrant Card in French Town." June 16:3.

———. 1995c. Celestine Bohlen. "Italy Rebuked by Vatican over Migrants." November 20:7.

Noiriel, Gérard. 1992. "Difficulties in French Historical Research on Immigration," in *Immigrants in Two Democracies: French and American Experience,* D. Horowitz and G. Noiriel (eds.). New York: New York University Press.

Oakley, Robin. 1992. "Report on Racial Violence and Harassment in Europe." (November 27). Strasbourg: Council of Europe.

Organisation for Economic Co-operation and Development (OECD). 1989. *Continuous Reporting System on Migration (SOPEMI), 1988.* Paris: OECD.

———. 1990. *Continuous Reporting System on Migration (SOPEMI), 1989.* Paris: OECD.

———. 1991. *Continuous Reporting System on Migration (SOPEMI), 1990.* Paris: OECD.

———. 1992. *Trends in International Migration. Continuous Reporting System on Migration (SOPEMI).* Paris: OECD.

———. 1994a. *Trends in International Migration, Annual Report 1993. Continuous Reporting System on Migration (SOPEMI).* Paris: OECD.

———. 1994b. "Italy's Report to SOPEMI." November 1994. (Prepublication version.)

———. 1994c. *OECD Economic Outlook.* 56. Paris: OECD.

———. 1995a. *Trends in International Migration, Annual Report 1994. Continuous Reporting System on Migration (SOPEMI).* Paris: OECD.

———. 1995b. "Italy's Report to SOPEMI." November 1995. (Pre-publication version.)

Papademetriou, Demetrios G. 1993a. "Confronting the Challenge of Transnational Migration: Domestic and International Responses" in *The Changing Course of International Migration.* Paris: OECD

———. 1993b. "Statement before the Subcommittee on International Law, Immigration and Refugees," in *Oversight Hearing on Employer Sanctions,* House Committee on the Judiciary, June 16, 1993. Washington, DC: Government Printing Office.

———. 1996. *The Faltering of European Integration: Migration and Related Issues.* Washington, DC: Carnegie Endowment for International Peace.

Papademetriou, Demetrios G., and Kimberly Hamilton. 1995. *Managing Uncertainty: Regulating Immigration Flows in Advanced Industrial Countries.* Washington, DC: Carnegie Endowment for International Peace.

Papademetriou, Demetrios G., and Stephen Yale-Loehr. 1996. *Putting the National Interest First: Rethinking the Selection of Skilled Immigrants.* Washington, DC: Carnegie Endowment for International Peace.

Papademetriou, Demetrios G., with Maryam Kamali Miyamoto. 1996. *Still a Study in Ambiguity: Germany and Immigration at the End of the Millenium.* Washington, DC: Carnegie Endowment for International Peace.

Pasqua, Charles. 1994. "Facing the Facts: An Evaluation of Immigration Policy," in *Harvard International Review.* (Summer):32-33.

Poulain, Michel. 1994. "Les flux migratoires dans le bassin mediterraneen," in *Politique Étrangère.* (Fall):689-705.

Presidential Commission on Nationality. 1988. *Être Français aujourd'hui et demain, Rapport rémis au Premier Ministre par Marceau Long.* Volume 1. Paris: Union Générale d'Editions.

Putnam, Robert. 1993. *Making Democracy Work.* New Jersey: Princeton University Press.

The Refugee Council. 1992. "UK Asylum Statistics: 1982-1992." Policy and Information Division. London: The Refugee Council.

Roche, T.W.E. 1969. *The Key in the Lock: Immigration Control in England from 1066 to the Present Day.* London: John Murray.

Salt, John. 1989. "International Migration and the United Kingdom: 1989 Report of the United Kingdom Correspondent to the SOPEMI Committee." University College London. (Pre-publication version.)

———.1991. "International Migration and the United Kingdom: Report of the United Kingdom SOPEMI Correspondent to the OECD, 1991." University College London. (Pre-publication version.)

———. 1992. "International Migration and the United Kingdom: Report of the United Kingdom SOPEMI Correspondent to the OECD, 1992." University College London. (Pre-publication version.)

———. 1993. "International Migration and the United Kingdom: Report of the United Kingdom SOPEMI Correspondent to the OECD, 1993." University College London. (Pre-publication version.)

———. 1994. "International Migration and the United Kingdom: Report of the United Kingdom SOPEMI Correspondent to the OECD, 1994." University College London. (Pre-publication version.)

———. 1995. "International Migration and the United Kingdom: Report of the United Kingdom SOPEMI Correspondent to the OECD, 1995." University College London. (Pre-publication version.)

Salt, John, and Ann Singleton. 1993. "The International Migration of Expertise: The Case of the United Kingdom." Paper presented at the International Seminar on Skilled and Highly Skilled Migration, Universita Pontina Latina. October 28-29.

Salt, John, Ann Singleton, and Jennifer Hogarth. 1994. *Europe's International Migrants: Data Sources, Patterns & Trends.* London: HMSO.

Secretariat of the Intergovernmental Consultations on Asylum, Refugee and Migration Policies in Europe, North America, and Australia (IGC). 1994. "Summary Description of Asylum Procedures in States in Europe, North America, and Australia" (June). Geneva.

Service d'Information et de Diffusion du Premier Ministre. 1994. *La lettre de Matignon,* No. 464, November 28. Paris.

Silberman, Roxane. 1992. "French Immigration Statistics," in *Immigrants in Two Democracies: French and American Experience,* Donald L. Horowitz and Gérard Noiriel (eds.). New York: New York University Press.

Silverman, Maxim. 1992. *Deconstructing Nation: Immigration, Racism and Citizenship in Modern France.* New York: Routledge.

Taguieff, Pierre-André (ed.). 1991. *Face au racisme.* (Volume 1, *Les moyens d'agir.*) Paris: Éditions la Découverte.

Tapinos, Georges. 1995. "The Socio-economic Challenges of Migration: Impacts on the Labour Market and Social Integration in Selected OECD Countries." Paper prepared for the OECD Conference on Migration and the Labour Market in Asia in the Year 2000, Tokyo, Japan. January 19-20.

Teitelbaum, Michael, and Jay M. Winter. 1985. *The Fear of Population Decline.* New York: Academic Press.

Thatcher, Margaret. 1995. "Identity Cards—Freedom under Threat." Text of a statement by former British Prime Minister Margaret Thatcher on behalf of Conservative Way Forward. (Undated.)

Tribalat, Michèle, Jean-Pierre Garson, Yann Moulier Boutang, and Roxane Silberman. 1991. *Cent ans d'immigration: Étrangers d'hier, Français d'aujourd'hui.* Paris: Institut National d'Études Démographiques.

United Kingdom Home Office. 1992. *Control of Immigration: Statistics, United Kingdom, 1991.* London: HMSO.

―――. 1994a. "Home Office Statistical Bulletin." London: Government Statistical Service. July 14.

―――. 1994b. *Control of Immigration: Statistics, United Kingdom, 1993.* London: HMSO.

―――. 1995a. "Home Office Statistical Bulletin.: London: Government Statistical Service. May 12.

―――. 1995b. *Immigration and Nationality Department (IND) Annual Report 1994.* London: HMSO.

U.S. Committee for Refugees (USCR). 1994. *World Refugee Survey 1994.* Washington, DC: U.S. Committee for Refugees.

―――. 1995. *World Refugee Survey 1995.* Washington, DC: U.S. Committee for Refugees.

U.S. Immigration & Naturalization Service (INS), Office of Policy & Planning. 1995. "Estimates of Undocumented Immigrant Population Residing in the United States by Country of Origin and State of Residence: October 1992," April 1995. Unpublished paper.

Vasta, Ellie. 1993. "Rights and Racism in a New Country of Immigration: The Italian Case," in *Racism and Migration in Western Europe,* John Solomos and John Wrench (eds.). Providence, RI: Berg Publishers.

Veil, Simone. 1994. "Forging Cultural Unity: Assimilation and Integration in France," in *Harvard International Review* (Summer):30-31.

Veugelers, John W.P. 1994. "Recent Immigration Politics in Italy: A Short Story," in *West European Politics* 17, No. 2 (April):33-49.

Weil, Patrick. 1994. Oral Remarks on "Adapting U.S. and French Immigration Policies to International Migration Pressures." A Seminar convened by U.S.-CREST in Washington, DC. October 4.

Weil, Patrick, and John Crowley. 1994. "Integration in Theory and Practice: A Comparison of France and Great Britain," in *West European Politics* 17, No. 2 (April):110-127.

Wihtol de Wenden, Catherine. 1993. "*Migrations et droits de l'homme,*" in *Le défi migratoire: Questions de rélations internationales.* Bertrand Badie and Catherine Wihtol de Wenden (eds.). Paris: *Fondation Nationale des Sciences Politiques*:159-178.

———. 1994. "The French Debate: Legal and Political Instruments to Promote Integration," in *European Migration in the Late Twentieth Century*, Heinz Fassmann and Rainer Münz (eds.). Aldershot, Hants, England: Edward Elgar Publishing, Ltd., for International Institute for Applied Systems Analysis (IIASA), Laxenburg, Austria.

ABOUT THE AUTHORS

DEMETRIOS G. PAPADEMETRIOU

Mr. Papademetriou is a Senior Associate of the Carnegie Endowment for International Peace and directs its International Migration Policy Program. He also serves as Chair of the Migration Committee of the Paris-based Organisation for Economic Co-operation and Development (OECD). His work concentrates on evaluating the adequacy of U.S. immigration policies and practices in meeting U.S. interests; the migration politics and policies of European and other advanced industrial societies; and the role of multilateral institutions in developing and coordinating collective responses to international population movements.

Mr. Papademetriou has published extensively in the United States and abroad on the immigration and refugee policies of the United States and other advanced industrial societies, the impact of legal and illegal immigration on the U.S. labor market, and the relationship between international migration and development. Prior to joining the Endowment, Mr. Papademetriou served as Director of Immigration Policy and Research at the U.S. Department of Labor and chaired the Secretary of Labor's Immigration Policy Task Force. Mr. Papademetriou has also served as Executive Editor of the *International Migration Review*. He has taught at Duke University, the University of Maryland, the Graduate Faculty of the New School of Social Research, and American University, where he is a recurring Scholar-in-Residence.

KIMBERLY A. HAMILTON

Kimberly A. Hamilton is pursuing a Ph.D. in Demography at Brown University, with a focus on international migration from Africa to Europe. From 1990 to 1994, she was on the staff of the Center for Strategic and International Studies (CSIS) in Washington, D.C., where she directed a project concerned with the "Security Dimensions of International Migration in Europe." As Associate Director of International Social Policy at CSIS, she was also responsible for research on the implications of population growth and HIV/AIDS. Ms. Hamilton received her M.A. from the Johns Hopkins University School of Advanced International Studies (SAIS) and her B.A. from the Robert D. Clark Honors College of the University of Oregon.

THE CARNEGIE ENDOWMENT FOR INTERNATIONAL PEACE

The Carnegie Endowment for International Peace was established in 1910 in Washington, D.C., with a gift from Andrew Carnegie. As a tax-exempt operating (not grant-making) foundation, the Endowment conducts programs of research, discussion, publication, and education in international affairs and U.S. foreign policy. The Endowment publishes the quarterly magazine, *Foreign Policy*.

Carnegie's senior associates—whose backgrounds include government, journalism, law, academia, and public affairs—bring to their work substantial first-hand experience in foreign policy through writing, public and media appearances, study groups, and conferences. Carnegie associates seek to invigorate and extend both expert and public discussion on a wide range of international issues, including worldwide migration, nuclear nonproliferation, regional conflicts, multilateralism, democracy-building, and the use of force. The Endowment also engages in and encourages projects designed to foster innovative contributions in international affairs.

In 1993, the Carnegie Endowment committed its resources to the establishment of a public policy research center in Moscow designed to promote intellectual collaboration among scholars and specialists in the United States, Russia, and other post-Soviet states. Together with the Endowment's associates in Washington, the center's staff of Russian and American specialists conduct programs on a broad range of major policy issues ranging from economic reform to civil-military relations. The Carnegie Moscow Center holds seminars, workshops, and study groups at which international participants from academia, government, journalism, the private sector, and nongovernmental institutions gather to exchange views. It also provides a forum for prominent international figures to present their views to informed Moscow audiences. Associates of the center also host seminars in Kiev on an equally broad set of topics.

The Endowment normally does not take institutional positions on public policy issues. It supports its activities principally from its own resources, supplemented by nongovernmental, philanthropic grants.

THE INTERNATIONAL MIGRATION POLICY PROGRAM

The movement of people has emerged as one of the critical issues facing the international community. Unless managed firmly but thoughtfully, migrations will pose critical challenges for democratic order and for international peace and stability. Against this backdrop, the International Migration Policy Program has developed a reputation as a leading source of expert analysis and policy ideas, as it focuses on bridging the worlds of immigration research and policy making and bringing an informed, independent voice to immigration policy debates here and abroad. The Program seeks to enhance the informed public's understanding of migration, refugee, and related topics and to shape the way policymakers think about and respond to these policy challenges. It does so by convening a series of breakfast briefings, luncheon seminars, policy roundtables, and study groups. Program staff also engage in an active schedule of writing and public speaking designed to promote a thoughtful and informed dialogue on this increasingly volatile policy area.

The Program also has convened an independent bilateral body, the U.S.-Mexico Consultative Group, to monitor and report on progress on cooperation in the areas of migration and labor within the NAFTA framework. Composed equally of U.S. and Mexican senior members of government, research, academic and advocacy organizations, the Consultative Group will candidly address the most intractable problems of border management and labor rights and standards.

The International Migration Policy Program receives funding for its activities from the Ford, MacArthur, Mellon, Sloan, and Tinker foundations.

Carnegie Endowment for International Peace
2400 N Street, N.W.,
Washington, D.C. 20037
Tel.: (202) 862-7900
Fax: (202) 862-2610
e-mail: ceip@igc.apc.org

Carnegie Moscow Center
Mosenka Plaza
24/27 Sadovaya-Samotechnaya
103051 Moscow, Russia
Tel: (7-095) 258-5025
Fax: (7-095) 258-5020
e-mail: carnegie@glas.apc.org

CARNEGIE ENDOWMENT FOR INTERNATIONAL PEACE OFFICERS AND BOARD OF TRUSTEES

Robert Carswell, Chairman of the Board
James C. Gaither, Vice Chairman of the Board
Morton I. Abramowitz, President
Paul Balaran, Vice President
Stephen R. Sestanovich, Vice President for Russian and Eurasian Affairs
Michael V. O'Hare, Secretary & Director of Finance and Administration

---

Morton I. Abramowitz
President,
Carnegie Endowment

Charles W. Bailey II
Journalist

Harry G. Barnes Jr.
Director,
Conflict Resolution and
Human Rights Program,
The Carter Center

Derek H. Burney
Chairman, President, and CEO,
Bell Canada International, Inc.

Robert Carswell
Of Counsel,
Shearman & Sterling

Gregory B. Craig
Partner,
Williams & Connolly

Richard A. Debs
Advisory Director,
Morgan Stanley International

William H. Donaldson
Donaldson Enterprises, Inc.

Marion R. Fremont-Smith
Partner,
Choate, Hall & Stewart

James C. Gaither
Partner,
Cooley, Godward, Castro,
Huddleson & Tatum

Leslie H. Gelb
President,
Council on Foreign Relations

Thomas L. Hughes
President Emeritus,
Carnegie Endowment

James A. Johnson
Chairman of the Board & CEO,
FannieMae

Donald Kennedy
President Emeritus and
Bing Professor of Environmental Science,
Stanford University,
Institute for International Studies

Robert Legvold
Professor of Political Science,
The Harriman Institute,
Columbia University

Wilbert J. LeMelle
President,
The Phelps Stokes Fund

Stephen R. Lewis, Jr.
President,
Carleton College

George C. Lodge
Professor,
Harvard University,
Graduate School of
Business Administration

Jessica Tuchman Mathews
Senior Fellow,
Council on Foreign Relations

Barbara W. Newell
Regents Professor,
Florida State University

Olara A. Otunnu
President,
International Peace Academy

Geneva Overholser
Ombudsman,
The Washington Post

Wesley W. Posvar
President Emeritus and
Professor of International Politics,
University of Pittsburgh

Edson W. Spencer
Spencer Associates

Charles J. Zwick
Retired Chairman,
Southeast Banking Corporation

A NEW CARNEGIE ENDOWMENT SERIES ON
INTERNATIONAL MIGRATION ISSUES

To contribute constructively to the policy debate on immigration in the United States and abroad—and to help deepen policymaker and public understanding of the migration and refugee situation worldwide—the International Migration Policy Program of the Carnegie Endowment for International Peace announces a new series of policy papers.

Three policy papers, listed below, are now available. Future issues focus on how the United States should select skilled immigrants; migration policy issues in Australia, Canada, Germany, and Japan; progress toward freedom of movement within the European Union; and the sources of modern conceptions of democratic citizenship.

1. MANAGING UNCERTAINTY:
Regulating Immigration Flows in Advanced Industrial Countries

Demetrios G. Papademetriou and Kimberly Hamilton identify and analyze the conceptual problems and principal issues involved in thinking about and developing contemporary immigration policy regimes. They argue that policymakers must develop immigration policies that are at once effective in dealing with changing world conditions, capable of reaping immigration's benefits, able to sustain public support, and consistent with international commitments.

ISBN 0-87003-069-8   Price: $ 5.95

2. U.S. REFUGEE POLICY:
Dilemmas and Directions

Kathleen Newland reviews four major elements of the U.S. refugee program—resettlement, temporary protection, first asylum, and emergency response—and argues that, as practiced, these do not add up to a coherent refugee *policy*. Minimizing the need for refugee protection should be the central thrust of post-Cold War U.S. refugee policy. Nonetheless, the difficulty of preventing or resolving refugee-producing conflicts means that robust U.S. leadership in providing protection is still urgently needed.

ISBN 0-87003-071-x   Price: $ 5.95

3. CONVERGING PATHS TO RESTRICTION:
French, Italian, and British Responses to Immigration

In this study, Demetrios G. Papademetriou and Kimberly Hamilton, focus on how France, Italy, and the United Kingdom are responding to the complex issues raised by immigration and asylum matters. They explore the often trial-and-error character of governmental responses to these issues, the absence of mainstream political-party leadership, and the growing disjuncture between initiatives motivated by increasingly restrictionist impulses and practical efforts to further the immigrant integration at the local level.

ISBN 0-87003-073-6 Price: $6.95

For credit card orders, call Carnegie's distributor, The Brookings Institution, toll-free at 1-800-275-1447; in Washington, D.C., call 202-797-6258. Fax: 202-797-6004. When ordering, please refer to code RVCC.